FEELING GOOD!

FEELING GOOD!

A Mental Health *Workbook*

DR. KOJO SARFO, DNP
@dr.kojosarfo

ADAMS MEDIA
New York London Toronto Sydney New Delhi

Adams Media
An Imprint of Simon & Schuster, Inc.
100 Technology Center Drive
Stoughton, Massachusetts 02072

First Adams Media trade paperback edition December 2022

Interior design by Priscilla Yuen
Interior images © Getty Images/Kumer; Simon & Schuster, Inc.

Manufactured in the United States of America

1 2022

ISBN 978-1-5072-1964-5
ISBN 978-1-5072-1965-2 (ebook)

ACKNOWLEDGMENTS

I want to thank my family and friends for supporting me and giving me the foundation to give my best to my patients and my online community. I wouldn't be here without the sacrifices that they've made, and I'm forever grateful for their patience and presence in my life. To my parents, Dr. Robert Sarfo and Jayne Sarfo, thank you for always being there. To my siblings, Christabel, Pius, Akosua, Amma, Kwame, and Robert Jr., thank you for giving me the confidence to be myself. And finally, to my online supporters, I want to say thank you so much for your support. Every follower matters, and I hope this book will help you realize that you're never alone and that there's always hope for a better tomorrow!

CONTENTS

Chapter 2

Chapter 3

Chapter 4

SADNESS / 94

Chapter 5

STRESS AND ANXIETY / 126

Chapter 6

CONFIDENCE / 148

Chapter 7

SOCIAL CONNECTIONS / 180

INTRODUCTION

Do you find yourself feeling down a lot?
Constantly stressing about work deadlines?
Freaking out that you said the wrong thing at that get-together?

If so, join the club. Many of us struggle to manage big emotions, quiet that never-ending stream of worries in our heads, and figure out what makes us happy. I have some good news: You don't have to feel sad and anxious all the time. *Feeling Good!* is here to help you prioritize and improve your mental health in simple, interactive ways.

Mental health impacts so many aspects of our lives—from our personal identity and self-confidence to our relationships to our ability to process emotions. A lot of us know how important mental health is, but how exactly do you go about improving it? With a little help from an expert and some self-reflection. That's right—there's no shame in asking for help, and that's what I'm here for. Actually, asking for help is, in my opinion, a *superpower*. It took me years to realize this, and it is my goal to simplify this process for you! By talking to a therapist, calling a friend, and filling out the pages in this workbook, you can find the support you need to feel better.

I was inspired to write *Feeling Good!* because I am on this journey as well, as an individual, healthcare provider, and mental health advocate. Yet I found that much of the information people hear about mental health is overwhelming, intimidating, and sometimes even scary. In *Feeling Good!*, I'm ditching the shame, fear, and confusion around mental health and boiling common challenges down to dozens of bite-sized exercises you can do in just a few minutes to address a wide range of issues. You'll gain a basic understanding of some common mental health concerns—such as low self-confidence, sadness, social anxiety, and stress—then learn some techniques for working through those issues. For example, you might need to set boundaries with a toxic friend, reframe negative thoughts, or schedule downtime so you're not overworked. Each exercise also offers an opportunity for you to reflect on how the topic applies to your life and brainstorm what steps you can take to overcome these challenges.

The ups and downs of life mean that mental health maintenance is something you need to think about every day, but it doesn't have to be a chore! With this workbook, you'll check in with yourself regularly through fun exercises that will help you address problems as they come up during everyday challenges. You have the power to reduce stress, manage sadness, boost self-confidence, and nurture relationships—and *Feeling Good!* will be there to guide you every step of the way.

HOW TO USE THIS BOOK

The goal of *Feeling Good!* is to teach you about important mental health topics and then help you figure out how to address them in your own life. Before we go any further, let me answer some questions about mental health that I hear often, such as, "What is mental health, anyway?" "Do you have to be diagnosed with a disorder in order to need therapy?" "How can you get help without feeling ashamed?" Read on to dispel some common myths and put yourself in the right frame of mind to begin the exercises.

What Is Mental Health?

Mental health refers to your ability to process your feelings and emotions and maintain a healthy well-being. Although many of us have a negative association with the term "mental health," it refers to a whole range of situations—just like physical health. Think of your mental health levels as a battery. Sometimes, you are fully charged and feel great. But at other times, you may notice yourself getting drained or not holding a charge like you used to. That may happen because of short-term mental health challenges, such as times of unusually high stress, lapses in self-confidence, and more. This book will help you focus on improving those things so that you can get yourself recharged.

When to Get Professional Help: Anytime!

We all experience sadness, self-doubt, and stress once in a while. However, if you find that issues like these are negatively affecting your day-to-day life—for example, you're unable to sleep, work, or focus—it's definitely time to see a professional. That said, you don't need to wait for situations to feel dire: You can and should see a mental health professional at any time for a checkup, just like you would for your physical health.

What's in a Diagnosis?

The majority of people in the United States will be diagnosed with a mental illness or disorder at some point in their lives. If that happens to you, take a deep breath. Think of the diagnosis as a formal way of being notified that you may need additional help in a certain area. A formal diagnosis can also give you specific guidance on tools that can help you feel like your best self again. Working with a professional is the best way to receive and manage a mental health diagnosis.

Even if you do not have a specific mental health diagnosis, regularly checking in on your mental health is an important tool for overall well-being.

Overcoming Stigma

Your mental health is just as important as your physical health. Unfortunately, there is a social stigma around mental health, which often prevents people from talking about it in a meaningful way. You may have experienced negative reactions to topics about mental health. Maybe someone didn't take your concerns seriously or made you feel ashamed about seeking help. Manifestations of this stigma—shame, embarrassment, and dismissal—are very real and can be challenging to overcome.

One way to overcome the stigma is simply to learn and talk about mental health like you would physical health. In this book, we'll leave the stigma behind and discuss topics that might be uncomfortable so that you can better understand and deal with them. After all, facing mental health head-on is the best way for everyone to feel seen, understood, and supported. Moving past the stigma of getting help for your mental health is an important step in your journey toward a better you.

Completing the Exercises

Feeling Good! is divided into chapters that address various common social and emotional topics. You can either work your way through the book page by page or jump around to topics that resonate with you on any given day.

In this workbook, you'll have an opportunity to learn more about mental health *and* yourself! Each exercise will:

- Explain a specific topic so that you understand how it can affect your mood, outlook, and mindset.
- Offer ideas and solutions that will empower you to change habits and beliefs that aren't working for you.
- Invite you to jot down some of your own experiences.
- Give you one or two small things you can do right away to help you feel better fast.

You can do these exercises at the same time every day (like right when you wake up or before you go to bed), or even a few times throughout the day when the mood strikes. You might want to revisit certain exercises as a refresher (if you find a particular challenge arising again) or as a reminder of the progress you've made. Grab extra paper for writing if you need it, and flag exercises that were particularly helpful. In short—use this book however it works best for you!

I hope that these exercises will feel like an interactive chat with me—and I'd love to hear about your progress. Find me @drkojosarfo on *Instagram/Facebook*, and @dr.kojosarfo on *TikTok*!

CHAPTER 1

YOU AND YOUR EMOTIONS

A question that I regularly ask my patients is, "How is your mood?" Depending on the day, your answer to that question may vary. It is normal for humans to experience the full range of emotions—everything from sadness and pain to elation and joy. As you feel these different emotions, you might find yourself confused, upset, or overwhelmed. Understanding what emotions you're experiencing and how to process them are the first steps toward good mental health, but most of us never learn how to do this! Yet without knowing how to process these feelings, you might find yourself being perpetually frustrated.

In this chapter, you will learn how to identify and process your emotions. As you do this, you'll also learn more about yourself and the world around you. Before we start, please understand that this work *will take time* and might be unsettling at first. You may realize that the reason your friendships struggle or you feel overwhelmed at school or work is because you are still working on establishing boundaries. You might notice that there are some parts of yourself that you aren't comfortable with at the moment. That's okay! Just by participating in this workbook, you are moving in the right direction. Keep going!

Who Am I?

Imagine that this is the first day of class and the teacher asks you to stand up, introduce yourself, and tell everyone a little bit about yourself. What would you say? How you describe yourself helps people understand what's important to you. It also tells people how you value yourself. If you're unsure of how to describe yourself, you might also feel unsure about your self-worth, talents, and best traits. Self-worth and self-acceptance are linked to mental health—you need to know who you really are in order to truly love and take care of yourself!

How to Manage This

Many of us don't slow down and take time to discover more about ourselves. Think back to introducing yourself to the class. After you said your name, what was the next thing you said about yourself? Was it something you think you are good at, maybe a hobby you enjoy? Understanding and valuing your identity is an important part of self-discovery and helps support your mental health. As you embark on this journey of mental wellness, it's important to become more self-aware to understand your wants and desires.

Write It Out

Who are you? What do you care about? These prompts will help you identify what you think of yourself and how you can convey that identity to other people.

What are your five most important traits?

1. ____________________
2. ____________________
3. ____________________
4. ____________________
5. ____________________

What are five things that you care about most deeply?

1. ______________________________

2. ______________________________

3. ______________________________

4. ______________________________

5. ______________________________

Now imagine a conversation in which you have to convey these traits and passions to a new friend. How would you let them know who you are? What words would you use to help them understand what matters most to you? Write how you would get those points across in conversation.

Action Steps

Knowing who you are can help you feel secure in your identity, value all your great qualities, and strengthen your confidence. Although this activity helped you brainstorm how others can learn more about you, I bet you learned something about yourself too. Is family the most important thing to you at this moment, or are your classes (or work) the most important for you currently? Do you value money or time more? You might want to revisit this exercise periodically as a self-discovery check-in to see what's changed as you grow and learn.

It's the Little Things

If I told you that there's a version of yourself that is happy, healthy, and thriving, would you even think that's possible? It is—and it doesn't have to feel overwhelming. The best thing about improving your mental health is that small, simple interventions go a long way! I want you to step into the next phase of your life—into a commitment to mental wellness. You can do this by taking small steps that will eventually add up to huge shifts in your mindset and health.

How to Manage This

Everyone has some small steps that they can take to become the best version of themselves. For example, I saw a huge shift in my confidence when I dedicated myself to eating breakfast and taking a walk every morning. *That's all!* Just those two changes allowed me to start my days with confidence, consistency, and momentum.

Write It Out

Consider the most difficult parts of your day or week. For example, do you struggle with waking up on time?

Difficult Parts of My Day or Week

Now use the following lines to write down some small steps you can take to address some or all of these issues. For example, if you're tired every morning, an earlier bedtime may help. It's okay to repeat some ideas on multiple days.

MONDAY ____________________

TUESDAY ____________________

WEDNESDAY

THURSDAY

FRIDAY

SATURDAY

SUNDAY

Action Steps

Going forward, try to implement just one or two steps every week to help you on your journey to becoming the best version of yourself. See if the small changes make challenging situations any less difficult, and make adjustments if needed. These small changes can support bigger changes later. Before you know it, you'll be on your way to actively managing your mental health...one step at a time.

Checking In on Myself

How often would you say that you "check in" on yourself? It may sound awkward, but pretend that you took your phone out to text yourself—the same way that you check in on friends. What would you say? You may have never thought of this in the past, and that's okay, because this isn't a thing that most people do—but you should! Forgetting to check in on your wants, needs, and overall well-being can leave you feeling unfulfilled or overwhelmed.

How to Manage This

Self-check-ins are a great practice that you can do, as often as needed. For example, on my morning walks I like to do a self-check-in to start the day. It is as simple as asking yourself questions like "How do I feel today?"; "What can I do to change or maintain those feelings?" Ask and "listen" to your body's response, just like you would with your best friend.

Write It Out

Now it's your turn. What are some ways that you can check in on yourself? Does my morning walk idea work for you? Maybe you're more of a night owl who likes to journal. Think about your busiest or most stressful times—be sure to check in on yourself then too. List a bunch of ideas here.

Action Steps

Now that you've determined ways you can check in on yourself, it is important to make this practice into a routine. Commit to doing a self-check-in at least every week—and aim for more often. Just as you perform lots of physical maintenance, such as exercising and showering, you need mental maintenance too. It is easy to get overwhelmed with the daily grind of responsibilities, but creating time to check in on yourself encourages you to focus on what your body and mind need at this moment. Maybe you need rest, motivation, or a helping hand—whatever it is, this check-in helps you get your needs met in order to feel better.

A Daily Emotion Tracker

It is important to understand how and why you feel the way you do. You know that your emotions can change based on what is going on in your life, but have you ever tracked your emotions and tried to find patterns or connect them to certain events? If you're too busy to pay attention to your feelings, you're missing the messages they're sending you. And being unaware of why you may suddenly feel happy or sad might cause feelings of confusion and stress. Those feelings could have lasting negative effects on your mental health.

How to Manage This

A good way to understand how you feel is by tracking your emotions over the course of a day, as you'll do in this exercise. Tracking your emotions allows you to become more aware of your feelings, when they occur, and what factors contribute to them. When you start to notice patterns around more challenging feelings—for example, that Monday morning meeting always stresses you out—you can work toward trying to address the underlying issue. Maybe assembling your materials Friday afternoon will help Monday morning feel less stressful. Conversely, you may realize that your time with a certain friend always leaves you feeling uplifted, energized, and happy. Plan more get-togethers with that friend!

Write It Out

Think about how you feel at this moment. Write down how you feel, when you started feeling this way, and how often you feel this way. Also, write down why you may be having this feeling. Feel free to copy and repeat this form or use another sheet of paper for additional days.

FEELING I OBSERVED	TIME OF DAY	HOW LONG IT LASTED	WHY I MIGHT HAVE FELT THIS WAY
Nervous	*9 a.m.*	*1 hour*	*I had an important meeting at 10 a.m. that I was worried about.*

FEELING I OBSERVED	TIME OF DAY	HOW LONG IT LASTED	WHY I MIGHT HAVE FELT THIS WAY

Action Steps

Examine the emotions you described. Do you understand why you felt a certain way and what caused the feeling? If you can draw parallels between your emotions and relevant factors in your life, you will gain insight into what makes you feel good—and what doesn't. This activity can help support your mental health by encouraging you to focus on activities that create positive emotions and reduce activities that may cause stress. Over the next month, try tracking your emotions as often as you can. See if you can slightly increase the number of times you feel happy and slightly reduce the number of times you feel a difficult emotion.

How to Feel Difficult Feelings

Have you ever tried to hide certain emotions? Maybe you went through a breakup and felt miserable or failed a big test and were simultaneously angry and disappointed. Think back to those situations. Did you feel like it was okay to feel and show those uncomfortable emotions? Many people hide difficult emotions from others...and even themselves. We may not feel well but choose to portray that everything is okay. That scenario hinders progress on your mental health journey. To stay in tune with yourself and your emotions, it's important to create an environment where it is okay to feel all of the emotions that you're going through.

How to Manage This

You may not hear this often, but it is okay to not feel okay. One of the most important parts of your journey to improved mental health is recognizing and allowing yourself to go through your feelings. Allow yourself time to process your emotions. Doing so gives you permission to accept whatever feeling you're going through. If you're miserable, it's okay to cry, listen to sad songs, or tell someone else that you're sad. Tell yourself that your feelings are valid, no matter what they are.

Write It Out

Think of a time when you felt like you had a safe space to "feel." Maybe you were surrounded by close friends or alone in your apartment. Perhaps you let out your feelings in words or went to a kickboxing class instead. Write down ways that you can create an environment where it is okay to "be" and "feel":

Action Steps

Now that you've written down ways you can create that safe space, consider ways to implement them in your daily life. Creating a safe environment to process your feelings should be one of your top priorities. It's important for you to feel safe during times when you feel the most vulnerable. Even though they're difficult, those times of vulnerability can help you grow. You learn that you can overcome hard times and get through to the other side, where you feel good.

Cancel Negative Self-Talk

Think about the way you speak to yourself when no one can hear you. Are you positive? Are you compassionate? Are you confident in yourself? If not, you are probably sending negative messages to yourself. This negative self-talk might affect the way you see yourself and the way you allow others to treat you. Negative thoughts might also put you in a bad mood, lower your confidence, and ruin your self-esteem. They might even make you second-guess every accomplishment or compliment you receive.

How to Manage This

A good way to manage negative self-talk is to transform the negative messages into positive ones. Think of how you'd talk to a friend—would you ever say some of the things you say to yourself to someone else? I doubt it. Start showing yourself the love and care you deserve by making sure that your self-talk is uplifting, encouraging, and reassuring.

Write It Out

List negative thoughts you tell yourself. For example, "I'm not smart enough to finish my degree"; "I'll never find a partner"; "I hate my body." Get these ugly statements out on paper so that we can work to rectify them.

Now let's transform each negative statement into something more positive. For example, "This work is hard, but I will finish my degree"; "I am worthy of love"; "My body does amazing things for me!"

Take a moment to reflect on both lists. I bet reading the positive statements helps you breathe easier, relax a bit, and smile. Those positive physical reactions will be reflected in your mental state as well—you'll feel less stressed, more confident, and happier when you speak to yourself in a positive way.

Action Steps

It's not unusual to have negative thoughts, but it is important to acknowledge them and try to change them. If you are constantly thinking about negative traits in yourself or your job or school, you're putting yourself down instead of building yourself up. Using positive statements instead will help you believe in yourself, reach your goals, and keep going. This habit may feel uncomfortable at first, but after some practice, it should feel easier to speak to yourself with positive words.

Avoid Knee-Jerk Reactions to Problems

Think about how you approach a problem. Do you immediately get angry or defensive, or shut down? Approaching problems in a way that's not constructive may negatively affect your mental health. It might also jeopardize your relationships with coworkers and friends. Jumping to conclusions or reacting without enough information can damage relationships and undo progress you've made on your mental health journey. Reacting badly to problems creates a negative experience for everyone...and tends to make a tough situation even worse.

How to Manage This

You can better manage how you approach problems by slowing down and trying to be levelheaded. When you're patient and calm, you can better analyze a situation before you react. Instead of freaking out, acknowledge that this problem is unfortunate, then calmly assess the damage and brainstorm how to work with others to provide a solution. This approach can save you from additional stress and damaging relationships with others.

Write It Out

Think back to one or two difficult situations you've had recently. Maybe someone hit your car in a parking lot, or a vendor was late with a big order you'd promised your best client. How did you respond? Write down how you felt and what you did (and be honest!).

Next, consider whether you could have done anything differently knowing what you know now about approaching problems. Write down what you've learned.

Action Steps

Don't be hard on yourself for any mistakes you made in the past—the key is to try to do better next time. In so many challenging scenarios, people run hot; they yell, name-call, or even get physical. Unfortunately, this approach usually just escalates the situation rather than resolving it—and it creates additional stress in your body and mind. Remember, it's better to calmly assess a situation before jumping in with strong emotions. Use what you've learned here to approach your next difficult situation in a way that solves the problem *and* benefits your mental health.

R-E-S-P-E-C-T

When you don't feel respected, your mental health suffers. You may feel insulted, ignored, or angry. These emotions can affect your daily life and how you approach relationships. Whether you are disrespected on purpose or by accident, it's important to let the person know that they hurt your feelings. If you remain silent about the ways you feel disrespected, the other person may never know how they offended you and might do it again. You are left harboring negative feelings that you never addressed.

How to Manage This

Understanding how you receive and accept respect is important. Once you understand the signals, words, or actions that register as respect to you, it's time to vocalize those preferences to those around you. For example, if you prefer public recognition for your work, that is your preference. Alternatively, if you don't like the attention and instead prefer a thoughtful email, that's your preference, which people should respect. Whatever the situation, the key is to communicate to others when something comes across as disrespectful to you.

Write It Out

First, think about times you've been disrespected. What happened? What feelings arose in you? Did you say anything at the time?

Now write about things that make you feel respected. Do people call you by your title, such as "doctor"? Do they ask how to pronounce your name?

Action Steps

Completing this activity will allow you the opportunity to acknowledge the ways you feel both disrespected and respected. Once you acknowledge the actions that feel respectful to you, consider how you can share that information with others so they know how to treat you. You can also try to practice these actions yourself when you're interacting with others. Doing so can help your personal relationships, as well as your professional, community, and other connections. You might also consider speaking up when someone does something disrespectful, so they know how you feel. Refer to How to Have a Difficult Conversation in Chapter 7 for ideas on how to have those discussions.

I Feel Most Loved When...

Think about what makes you feel loved. Is it a soft touch? Appreciation? Little acts of kindness? We all accept and receive love differently, but many of us do not always voice how we prefer to receive that love. It is important to learn to be aware of your needs so you can communicate them to others—and be sure you are getting what you need from yourself as well.

How to Manage This

Take some time to figure out what makes you feel loved. For example, "I feel the most loved when I am heard. It's important for me to feel that people around me are listening to me and valuing my needs. By understanding this, my loved ones listen to me, creating a strong connection that supports feelings of love." Once you know what works for you, you can share that information with loved ones and use it in self-check-ins to make sure you are showing yourself that love as well.

Write It Out

In this activity, you will fill in the blanks and describe when and how you feel most loved. Consider all the ways you feel loved, large or small.

Action Steps

Consider the list you just made. Did anything surprise you? Do you do any of these actions for yourself? If not, now is a great time to start. Remember, it's as important for *you* to understand how you receive and accept love as it is for other people to know that. Knowing what love looks like to you will also help you feel more confident in your relationship decisions. Soon, you'll be more comfortable talking about your needs and advocating for yourself when necessary.

Recognizing My Limits

Have you heard the phrase "push yourself to the limit" or "I'll sleep when I'm dead"? In today's busy world, people are often encouraged to push themselves to (or past!) the breaking point to achieve success. However, this is one of the top reasons many people struggle with mental health. We are not made to have infinite limits. Pushing yourself to the end of your rope is not healthy. It can cause chronic stress, feelings of frustration or dissatisfaction, and burnout. Plus, overdoing it can affect your physical well-being—you might experience muscle tension, fatigue, insomnia, or headaches.

How to Manage This

It's important to recognize your limits and rest when your mind and body tell you. You can recognize your limits by paying attention to how you feel and opening yourself up to feedback from others. Listen to your body: Are you always exhausted? Struggling to focus? You probably need rest. Understanding what you can and cannot do will allow you to respect your physical and mental health. It can also prevent burnout by allowing you to place yourself in positions that enable you to win.

Write It Out

How do you know when you're reaching your limit? Write down some examples that show you're approaching your limit. For example, "I become forgetful"; "I become anxious"; "I am impatient."

Now brainstorm some ways you can respect those limits better in the future. For example, you might commit to only one weeknight activity or aim to get a certain number of hours of sleep each night.

Action Steps

Now that you've written down examples, you should have a better idea of where your limits are and how to respect them and take a break. It's up to you to determine what that break looks like, whether it's a day off or seeking professional support. The goal is for you to better understand the cues that help you manage your stress before it affects your mental health by causing burnout or depression. Pay attention to the cues and make decisions that prioritize your mental health.

Pencil In Peace

Living in a chaotic environment 24/7 is not good for anyone. Sure, we're all busy, but we also need downtime. Yet many of us aren't sure how to relax anymore! We might fill any empty spots in our schedule with screen time, more get-togethers, or even more work. When you don't prioritize some peace and quiet, you can experience burnout, exhaustion, and a constant stream of worries in your head. These are heavy consequences for neglecting your need for peace.

How to Manage This

Finding true peace is a lost art, but you can reclaim it by penciling in peace. A lot of the exercises in this book will help you. Whether you need help wrangling your busy schedule (check out Managing Day-to-Day Activities and Creating Short-Term Mental Health Goals, both in Chapter 2), pushing back on requests when you need to (try How to Say No in Chapter 2, and Setting Healthy Boundaries in Chapter 7), or knowing what makes you happy (see Looking for Hidden Opportunities to Focus On Me in Chapter 2, and Savoring Happiness Wherever, Whenever! in Chapter 3), you will have lots of tools for opening up space in your day for peace and doing things you like.

Write It Out

What does true peace look like to you? In the space here, write down keywords and phrases that represent peace, including locations and how your five senses are engaged. For example, you may write about being on a beach or at the spa, or enjoying your favorite tea.

Action Steps

Now that you have described activities or things that are peaceful to you, consider how you can integrate those into your life on a regular basis. We all deal with stress in our personal and work relationships, but it's important for you to manage those stressors by balancing them with opportunities to feel at peace. As you continue your mental health journey, you'll find that managing situations and prioritizing what makes you feel at peace can create a better life balance.

Measuring My Progress

Working to improve your mental health is such an important job, but it doesn't happen overnight. You're doing a great job so far! Remember that you are doing something that is very difficult. Many people avoid challenges, but you are here doing the work. Sitting down with your uncomfortable feelings can be a tricky thing—after all, bringing your feelings to the forefront might make you feel vulnerable or afraid. Still, it's important to keep moving forward and be proud of your progress.

How to Manage This

You've come through the first chapter and made a tremendous amount of progress! This is a good time to look back at how much you've grown in your mental health journey. Think about where you were at the beginning of the book and where you are now. Take time to measure your progress and applaud your growth! Celebrating each step in your journey will help you stay motivated and eager to keep going.

Write It Out

Write down ways your mental health has progressed since you began this workbook. Think about activities that have really helped you progress.

Action Steps

As you move forward in this book, it is important that you continue to evaluate and celebrate your progress during this journey. These reflections put what you've learned and how you've incorporated your new skills at the front of your mind. It is also important that you recognize the growth you have achieved. And it is all because you wanted to improve your mental well-being on your own. That takes a tremendous amount of courage, and you should be proud of yourself!

CHAPTER 2

VALUES AND PRIORITIES

Your values and priorities are key parts of what makes you, you. You can decide what your values and priorities are after you spend some time thinking hard about what matters to you, what makes you truly happy, what inspires you, what activities will improve your life, and what you want to achieve now and in the future. Identifying your values and priorities is an important step on your mental health journey because you can then focus on the people and activities that deserve your time, based on your choices. You'll likely feel happier and less stressed if you spend most of your time doing things you want to do with people you like. Plus, with the time you save not doing things you don't want to do, you can create *more* opportunities to do the things that matter most to you.

In this chapter, we will focus on activities that can help you determine your priorities, values, and goals. You'll discover methods to help you better recognize where you spend your time and how you currently manage your priorities: Are you focusing on the things that really matter to you? You will also learn how prioritizing, or failing to prioritize, can affect your mental health. Along the way, you'll create action steps to help you set your priorities and concentrate on what's important to you.

What Is Most Important to Me?

Do you ever go through your day without really stopping to think about how you're spending your time? It's very helpful to take a few moments to figure out the most important aspects of your day so that you can focus on executing those priorities first and foremost. Becoming aware of where your time and energy are going can help you organize yourself and reduce burnout and stress. Instead of feeling weighed down by things that are not very important in the moment, you can give your best self to the people and tasks that are the highest priority to you. Focusing on getting a few tasks done well every day will help you feel more fulfilled and accomplished than trying to do too many of them halfway.

How to Manage This

I recognize that I cannot do everything in a day, but I can do *anything* in a day. That is, I understand which activities I need to focus on right now and which ones I can do on another day. This recognition opens up my schedule, allowing me to do multiple things in one day—without the pressure of feeling like I have to get everything done. Adopting this thinking will put you in a much better position to achieve your priority tasks and reduce stress along the way.

Write It Out

For this activity, we'll think "in themes" instead of in terms of specific to-do items. In the spaces here, list all the categories of responsibilities that you cover on a regular basis. Here are some ideas to get you started and space to write in your own. In the right-hand column, list the number of hours per week you spend doing that activity.

TASK	TIME SPENT PER WEEK
Grocery shopping	
Work	
Childcare	

TASK	TIME SPENT PER WEEK
Care of a parent/other family member	
Paying bills	
Food preparation	
Housecleaning	
Laundry	

Now circle the top three to five categories that are most important to you. If you're not sure, imagine that you were really pressed for time. Which categories would rise to the top as being crucial for you to tend to?

Action Steps

Circling and identifying the priority items will illustrate what you define as your most important activities at that moment. This process is building recognition about what is most important for you to have a successful day. It helps you determine which tasks are your priority so that your focus lives there. You can then move through your day without having an overwhelming amount of stress. You might also realize how much time certain responsibilities are taking up—and you might want to consider other options to get these tasks done (see Do I Need Help? in Chapter 3 for ideas).

Managing Day-to-Day Activities

Taking the dog for a walk. Making dinner. Going to work. Doing laundry.... Daily to-do lists can get overwhelming fast. What does that have to do with your mental health? If you feel like you're drowning in your day-to-day activities, you might experience burnout, stress, and even depression. Plus, it's no fun to always feel like you're running around frantically and *still* not getting everything done. Many of these issues can be avoided, or at least managed, with better organization.

How to Manage This

Planning helps you pace yourself, make your time count, prepare for daily challenges, and minimize stress inducers. One method I like to use is listing my goals for the day. I call it my "plan of attack." I check off each goal as I complete it. If I don't have time to complete a goal, I add it to the next day's plan. This is an easy way to monitor your time and complete tasks. You'll feel accomplished each time you check off an item, but the goal is to learn how to manage your daily activities. If you frequently have to move a less time-sensitive task to another day, that's fine—but it probably means you're trying to take on too much.

Write It Out

In this activity, you will create a list of three goals for each day this week and list them in order of priority. These don't need to be epic, life-changing goals—"get myself to work on time" is a great goal. "Make a healthy lunch instead of grabbing fast food" is another option. Make them attainable.

MONDAY	1. 2. 3.
TUESDAY	1. 2. 3.
WEDNESDAY	1. 2. 3.

THURSDAY	1. 2. 3.
FRIDAY	1. 2. 3.
SATURDAY	1. 2. 3.
SUNDAY	1. 2. 3.

At the end of the week, reflect on how you did. Which goals were easiest to finish? Which kept getting pushed to another day? Why?

Action Steps

Setting achievable goals each day will help you feel accomplished, understand where your time is going, and avoid taking on too much. Plus, writing down your goals can prevent you from feeling overwhelmed or anxious that you're forgetting things. Remember, managing your day is *not* about doing as much as you possibly can from dawn to dusk. The most important thing is to take on only what you can handle, do those tasks well, and enjoy any leftover free time!

Add Time Buffers

It is unrealistic to assume that you can complete everything that you want to do all the time. Having unrealistic expectations and not living up to them will cause frustration. That frustration may eventually manifest itself in negative mental health consequences, such as anxiety, stress, or depression. It is healthier to understand how much really needs to be done and the time frame you are working with. If you find that you're always running out of time or having trouble managing your time, it may mean that you're overscheduling activities or underestimating your time.

How to Manage This

One very effective method for avoiding time underestimation is to create "time buffers." These are extra pockets of time that you schedule to give yourself more time than usual on a task or activity. We often underestimate how long a drive will take or how long the line will be at the grocery store. Once you start planning extra for those periods of time, you'll find that your daily plans will be more realistic and doable.

Write It Out

In this activity, you'll recap your day. Think about the things you did today, the time you think it takes to complete each task, and how long it actually took. Reflect on how the task went and how it could have gone better. Some example tasks are provided for you.

TASK	TIME I THOUGHT I'D SPEND	ACTUAL TIME SPENT	REFLECTION
Morning routine	*1 hour*	*1 hour 10 minutes*	*I spend a lot of time trying to get out of the house. I'm always running late, and it makes me feel stressed and unprepared for the day. Going forward, I'll collect my things the night before, so they are ready to go in the morning.*

TASK	TIME I THOUGHT I'D SPEND	ACTUAL TIME SPENT	REFLECTION
Grocery shopping	*45 minutes*	*1 hour*	*The line is always so long if I go midday on a weekend. I plan as if I will just run in quickly, but it takes longer than I think it will. I need to add extra time if I go on a weekend.*

The difference between the time you spent and the time you thought you'd spend is that buffer time you need to add.

Action Steps

You can see how small pockets of buffer time really add up over the course of a day. Even if you do one or two fewer tasks because of this buffer time, your day will run much more smoothly and you're likely to feel less stressed, more in control, and happier. Try adding buffer time this week—it can be as simple as assuming a drive will take an hour if your map app says it'll take fifty minutes. That way, if you hit a bit of traffic or it takes you a few minutes to find a parking spot, you won't be late. (Tip: If you *do* arrive in fifty minutes, use that extra ten minutes for self-care—see Looking for Hidden Opportunities to Focus On Me, later in this chapter, for more information.)

Stop Mindless Scrolling Forever!

The Internet can be so amazing. We can search for almost limitless information, go shopping, connect with friends, and catch the latest viral videos. However, there are downsides to spending endless hours on your phone that might affect your mental well-being. Scrolling mindlessly—without a clear goal—puts you at risk for such things as anxiety, depression, and stress because of the sometimes addictive nature of certain apps and websites. For example, studies have shown how addictive notifications and interactions from social media can be—you want to immediately check what just came in. Plus, many people compare their bodies or their lives to other people's social media pictures, and might start criticizing themselves as a result. Those behaviors may lead to negative impacts on your mental health.

How to Manage This

Trying to get a handle on your Internet usage isn't easy, as it's usually within arm's reach all day. But you *can* learn to manage your usage. For example, you could set a timer before you go on certain apps that you may find addictive. As a full-time content creator, I have to be on the Internet for my job, but I'm still very careful about managing my time and the type of content I take in. Understanding your own Internet habits, as we'll do in this exercise, will help you become more aware of what healthy Internet usage looks like for you.

Write It Out

Write down how much time you spend on each social media app and websites that you visit every day. You can get an app that helps you with this task or see if your smartphone already tracks your usage. Be sure to note your mood after you finish using the app or visiting the site. Are you uplifted and energized, or angry and feeling left out? Record what you observe.

APP/SITE	TOTAL TIME SPENT	HOW IT MAKES ME FEEL

APP/SITE	TOTAL TIME SPENT	HOW IT MAKES ME FEEL

Now reflect on what you discovered. Did any of the numbers surprise you? Did you realize that certain apps or sites were making you feel a certain way?

Action Steps

By tracking your daily Internet usage and recognizing how that usage makes you feel, you can begin to structure healthier Internet habits. Consider how you use the Internet and work toward more purposeful interaction. For example, if following certain people on social media regularly makes you feel bad about yourself, try unfollowing or muting them. If checking in with your favorite motivational content creator helps you start your day strong, look at their posts first thing in the morning. This type of intentional Internet use can help you feel happier and more empowered.

How to Say No

It's important for you to know your value. Knowing your values and worth is part of setting boundaries, prioritizing your needs, and teaching people how to treat you. Sometimes your time is worth more than a task someone wants you to do. In these cases, you will have to tell people "no." Learning to say no can be difficult, but it's necessary. "No" does not mean you have ill feelings toward anyone or that you can never, ever do that task; it is just realizing that you are not in a place to accommodate their request at this time. Having the confidence to say no—and stand firm in your decision—is an important way to value your sense of self, your time, and your priorities.

How to Manage This

I enjoy helping people. I find it gratifying. However, I realize that my time is also very valuable. I can't say yes to every request I get. Outside of emergencies, I do not allow people to make last-minute requests of my time. You can create boundaries by managing people's expectations of your time. Set a time limit, push back on a request, or simply say no to requests that impede your plans. This response not only sets boundaries but also helps increase your confidence and reduce stress over time. You don't need to launch into long explanations or apologies—a response like "Thank you for thinking of me, but I can't help this time" works well. Also, in a pinch, say, "Let me think about that and let you know later." That buys you some time to consider the request without feeling pressured or rushed.

Write It Out

Practicing saying no ahead of time can be very helpful. For this exercise, think about requests that you agreed to do even though you really didn't have the time or interest. In the boxes here, write down how you could respond to the first two requests if you didn't want to do them. In the blank boxes, write down other common requests that you receive and how you could say no to them.

REQUEST	HOW YOU COULD SAY NO
I know you just got off a long shift at work, but can you swing by the store and pick up a few items I forgot?	
Thanks so much for lending a hand the last few weeks planning the fundraiser. We were wondering if you'd come to the event this weekend too and help us for a few hours more.	

Examine the responses you just wrote. How do you feel about them? If you usually say yes to everything, saying no will likely feel uncomfortable at first. Try to release feelings of guilt and remind yourself that you are managing your time in order to prioritize your physical and mental health.

Action Steps

The goal of the exercise is to get into the practice of setting a boundary and telling people that you cannot accommodate them. Remember, you want to be firm and confident, but it's also good to be gracious. The people receiving the message may not like your response, but you must remember that you are not responding with ill intentions. This process will help you set boundaries that honor your values, feelings, and time so that you can focus on self-care.

Looking for Hidden Opportunities to Focus On Me

When it comes to managing your time, setting priorities, and putting yourself first, you may find that getting started can be challenging. The good news is that you can find small pockets of time here and there to relax, recharge, and rest. If you constantly run yourself ragged, you'll be overtired, more impatient, and unhappy. Putting your mental health first can look like taking a few breaks during your day to focus on how you're feeling and what you need.

How to Manage This

You may not be used to prioritizing yourself or your needs; however, this is the perfect time to start. Look for short opportunities during the day to focus on yourself. They may show up as a peaceful walk before heading home from work or making a spa appointment when a client cancels a meeting at the last minute. These hidden opportunities are great times for self-care. Once you get the hang of creating purpose in these hidden opportunities, you'll find it easier to continue making time for yourself. Remember, this is not a "guilty pleasure" situation—this is hard-earned, well-deserved time for yourself!

Write It Out

Think about times when you should have prioritized your needs, but for whatever reason, you didn't. Look over the following list and check any reasons you may have neglected your needs. Feel free to add reasons that are not listed.

❑ Too busy	❑ ______________________
❑ Habitually forget about my needs	❑ ______________________
❑ Too tired	❑ ______________________
❑ Family priorities	❑ ______________________
❑ Couldn't afford it	❑ ______________________
❑ Work priorities	❑ ______________________

Now take some time to list "hidden" ways for you to capture time for self-care in the future. Think about your day and try to find ten- or fifteen-minute chunks of time you could use for yourself. Can you reduce your phone time by fifteen minutes and instead take a walk around a nearby park? What about actually taking the coffee and lunch breaks you're supposed to get at work? List these blocks of hidden time and what you could do during them.

Action Steps

Remember, your self-care, needs, and priorities matter. Even when it feels like your schedule is packed, be on the lookout for short periods of time you can use to do something nice for yourself. Try to find one ten-minute block every day—you'll be amazed at the difference it can make to your mood and happiness!

Creating Long-Term Mental Health Goals

You are on a mental health journey. The journey will be long and winding, but I promise it will be rewarding. Part of that journey is figuring out what your long-term mental health goals look like. These are goals that may take a few weeks or even years to accomplish. Goals that take years are the "endgame," big-picture aspirations that encompass several smaller goals through the years. Examples include avoiding negative self-talk, prioritizing self-care, and achieving or maintaining sobriety. Having long-term mental health goals can help you stay focused on what's ahead and create a path toward reaching happiness and success, however you define them.

How to Manage This

In brainstorming long-term goals, start small. I take a few minutes to really check in on myself and figure out what I would like to change about my life. I am very busy, and I recognize that I need more rest. Now I prioritize rest, and I make sure that I get what I need to recalibrate. Focusing on this one goal helps so many areas of my life. You can manage long-term goals by checking on your progress a few times a month.

Write It Out

Don't let the idea of "long-term mental health goals" be intimidating or overwhelming. For the first part of this exercise, brainstorm five benchmarks that you use to deem yourself healthy. For example, "I am getting a good night's sleep regularly," "I write in my journal as part of my morning routine," "I have friends I really connect with," and "I find time to exercise three days a week." It's okay if you're not currently doing all these things perfectly. For now, just describe what a healthy you looks and feels like.

1. ______________________________

____

2. ______________________________

____

3. ____________________

____

4. ____________________

____

5. ____________________

____

Now think about whether there is a long-term goal or two that you could build out of these benchmarks. For example, can you aim to sleep seven hours every night?

1. ____________________

____

2. ____________________

____

Action Steps

The items you've identified on that first list are important parts of your mental health journey. For the things that you are currently doing well, are those things that you would have said before focusing on your mental health? If not, that is a mark of change in you that you should celebrate! For those areas that you still want to work on, congratulate yourself on discovering them. Becoming aware of things you want to change is the first step toward improving them. Aim to make a little progress on your long-term goals each month. The next exercise will help you do that.

Creating Short-Term Mental Health Goals

Short-term mental health goals are just as important as long-term ones. These can be daily tasks or weekly goals. Think of them as brief sprints toward that far-away finish line—each one gets you a bit closer, even if you walk for a while in between them. Short-term goals help you complete tasks in a timely manner and keep you on track for your bigger goal. For example, being able to make it through one day without believing negative thoughts about yourself is a great short-term goal on the way to eliminating negative thoughts about yourself as often as possible. Knowing that you are able to complete these smaller goals can improve your confidence, boost your mood, and motivate you to keep working toward that larger goal or plan.

How to Manage This

You can manage short-term goals in a few ways. One way is having a support friend or accountability partner. This person will check in to make sure you're sticking to the plan and taking care of yourself. You can also create quick tasks to complete before reaching your short-term goal. Try adding these small tasks to your task or note app in your smartphone. Check them off as you complete them, even if they don't take long. When you check off tasks, your self-esteem will improve, you'll avoid burnout, and you'll stay motivated.

Write It Out

What are some short-term mental health goals that you've accomplished recently? Write up to fifteen short-term goals in the space here. Reflect on the steps you took to accomplish these goals. Maybe you said no to a few requests, or you minimized judgmental thoughts.

SHORT-TERM GOALS I'VE ACCOMPLISHED

1. ______________________________

____

2. ______________________________

____

3. ______________________________

____

4. ______________________________

____

5. ______________________________

____

6. ______________________________

____

7. ______________________________

____

8. ______________________________

____

9. ______________________________

____

10. ______________________________

____

11. ______________________________

____

12. ______________________________

____

13. ____

____

14. ____

____

15. ____

____

How did you accomplish these goals? Maybe you practiced saying no in your head, or observed your judgmental thoughts when they arose and just let them go. Write down a few ways you reached these goals.

Now review the long-term goals you brainstormed in the last exercise. Choose one to start now. Write up to five short-term goals to help you achieve the long-term one. Break the process down into small parts as much as possible.

LONG-TERM GOAL TO WORK ON

SHORT-TERM GOALS TO WORK ON

1. ______________________________

____

2. ______________________________

____

3. ______________________________

____

4. ______________________________

____

5. ______________________________

____

Action Steps

Setting and achieving short-term goals is a great way to stay focused on your mental health as you go about your busy life. Be sure to celebrate every step of your journey in a meaningful way. When you check off a short-term goal, indulge in a special treat that you enjoy. You should take a lot of pride in what you are accomplishing!

Living My Passions

One special way to "feel good" is to be of service to someone or something else. That's right—giving your time or energy to a cause can have a positive impact on *your* mental health. You'll boost your confidence, feel proud of your contributions, and share your enthusiasm for the project, all while making the world a better place. Whether it's fostering shelter animals, protecting the environment, political activism, or some other cause, consider making volunteer work a part of your regular self-care practices.

How to Manage This

Try to find a way that you can contribute to a cause that's important to you. If you're short on money, donate your time and energy. If you currently have no time but a few extra dollars, make a monetary contribution. Or maybe you have a talent you can share. For example, if you're an accountant, offer to keep the books for a local nonprofit organization. Are you great at social media? Offer to make engaging posts for your cause. Either way, helping advance a cause will leave you feeling empowered, important, and fulfilled. When I make an intentional effort to improve someone else's day, there's a noticeable boost in my mood that day too!

Write It Out

In this activity, think about how, where, and when you could be of service. Your commitments can be short or long term, and in the form of time, efforts, talents, or money. One example is provided.

CAUSE	PERSONAL PASSIONS IT RELATES TO	HOW I COULD HELP	WHEN I COULD VOLUNTEER
Local park cleanup	*My love of the environment and my neighborhood*	*Buy trash bags and gloves and pick up garbage*	*The first weekend of every month in the summer*

CAUSE	PERSONAL PASSIONS IT RELATES TO	HOW I COULD HELP	WHEN I COULD VOLUNTEER

Action Steps

Look over your list of ideas and implement one during the next month. Even better, see if you can get a friend to join you. That way, you've made it a social event too. Your passions are an important part of your identity—sharing your excitement for a cause is a great way to let your light shine onto the world!

CHAPTER 3
SELF-LOVE

Loving yourself seems like a no-brainer, but many of us struggle with this idea. The concept can make some people feel selfish or self-absorbed, and others have a hard time finding things to love about themselves. This sad state of affairs has a huge impact on your mental health. Although the mass media and society at large have a big influence on how you perceive yourself, the messages you tell yourself are even more important. Are you treating your body and mind with the love and respect they deserve? Do you believe you are capable of greatness? Self-love is all about appreciating yourself for who you are—just as you are, right now.

Surprisingly, self-love can also improve all of your relationships too. Practicing self-love helps you be a better partner and friend because you'll be able to create and receive positive interactions with loved ones and handle disagreement and disappointment better in the workplace. Self-love also affords more confidence in your interactions with others and your ability to create boundaries and prioritize your needs.

The following exercises will help you create more positivity in your life, manage feelings about yourself, and complete activities that aim to promote a strong appreciation and love of self. These activities will help you make practicing self-love an everyday habit.

What Does Self-Love Mean to Me?

Figuring out ways to love yourself is crucial when it comes to maintaining your mental health. The occasional negative feelings we all have about ourselves do not matter as much when you love the person that you are. You may take a while to feel comfortable loving yourself, but it's worth the time and effort. Loving yourself can also help ward off feelings of depression, insecurity, anxiety, and so much more.

How to Manage This

One of the ways I like to promote self-love is by asking myself what I need to prosper in this moment. Sometimes that is getting more sleep or going to the gym more often. Sometimes it is as simple as stepping outside a loud area to get a moment of peace and quiet. Loving yourself can be a fun activity, and you can do it in many ways. It's up to you to find the best ways to love yourself.

Write It Out

Try to define what self-love means to you. To do that, let's start by writing down five ways you show love to someone dear to you—whether it's a romantic partner, family member, or close friend.

1. ______________________________

____

2. ______________________________

____

3. ______________________________

____

4. ______________________________

____

5. ____

____

Now turn the tables and think of five ways you put yourself first and express love for yourself.

1. ____

____

2. ____

____

3. ____

____

4. ____

____

5. ____

____

Finally, reflect on the two lists. Which was more difficult to fill out? Many people find it considerably harder to think of kind things they do *for themselves*—but that is just as important as the love you show others!

Action Steps

Look at the second list you made and try each item one at a time over the course of a week. The goal is to show appreciation for yourself, so these should be things that you enjoy and look forward to. Try them at different times—for example, try one when you need an energizing pick-me-up; try another when you need to rest and recharge. See how they work in different situations and how you feel afterward. The more ways you try, the more likely you will find something useful in different situations.

Write Down Daily Affirmations

The things that you say to yourself affect your well-being in various ways. You'd probably feel sad, hurt, or even humiliated if someone else told you that you weren't smart or that some part of your body was ugly. The result is the same when you're the one spreading those types of negative messages internally. Being able to see yourself in a positive light is a cornerstone for good mental health. It feeds into your confidence, which helps with so much on this journey. Making a habit of thinking of positive thoughts about yourself is a very effective way to practice self-love.

How to Manage This

Instead of putting yourself down, create positive feelings by reframing your thoughts. This simple reframing will help you feel so much better about yourself. A great way to do this is by speaking highly of yourself, just like you would talk about a good friend. I like to pretend I am someone close to me, like my best friend, and talk as if I were speaking to me. I'm not as conscious about flattery when I'm pretending to be someone else. Try starting your day by looking in the mirror and telling yourself how special you are. It may feel uncomfortable at first, but the more you do it, the easier it will be. Keep going!

Write It Out

For this activity, write six positive things you feel about yourself. Don't worry too much about the wording at this point—just capture key positive feelings. For example, "I am really proud of how I get up and exercise four days a week," or "I am great with my nieces and nephews."

POSITIVE THINGS ABOUT ME

Now transform those statements into short, present-tense affirmations that celebrate the best parts of yourself. For example, you could write, "My body is strong and powerful," or "I am kind and compassionate."

POSITIVE AFFIRMATIONS

Action Steps

Write some of your favorite affirmations on sticky notes and post them on your mirror. When you wake up, read the notes aloud. Or stick them by your front door or your work computer. No matter how it is done, repeating positive self-affirmation is a healthy way to practice self-love. Be sure to revisit your list and think of new affirmations to add daily or monthly. The key is to see these thoughts every day and keep them at the front of your mind.

Practicing Self-Acceptance

Sometimes it is difficult for people to accept part or all of themselves. You may feel ashamed, embarrassed, or uncomfortable with one of your personality traits, interests, or goals. These feelings can cause anxiety, low self-confidence, and even depression. Everyone has faults and things about themselves that they want to improve, and growth and change are healthy. But allowing those insecurities to dictate how you feel about yourself only leads to poor mental health.

How to Manage This

You can practice self-acceptance by learning to appreciate who you are right now. I know that there is something special about you! For example, I have attention-deficit/hyperactivity disorder (ADHD), and as a child I thought it held me back. I didn't want to accept that part of me. Now that I have the appropriate resources and tools around me, I like to think that sometimes my ADHD actually *helps* me with creativity and inspiration. It may take time, but acknowledging every trait or difference can help you become more self-confident, and it is the first step in practicing self-acceptance.

Write It Out

You have probably thought many times about all the things you'd change about yourself if you could. For this exercise, let's switch it up and write down eight things you *cannot* change. In the right-hand column, describe how you work through these things in your daily interactions.

THING I CANNOT CHANGE	HOW I WORK THROUGH IT
I wish I were taller.	*I spend time finding ways to be comfortable living life at my height.*

THING I CANNOT CHANGE	HOW I WORK THROUGH IT

Now reflect on the things you wrote that you cannot change. How many of them were negative versus positive? Focus on the negative descriptions. How can you reword these to be more positive? For example, could you say, "I accept my height," or "I am the right height for me"?

Action Steps

Practicing self-acceptance is all about embracing what you perceive to be negative about yourself. Loving all parts of yourself is an important part of self-love. Learning to accept things you think are negative can be a long process, but the work you did in this exercise is an effective way to change your perception of what's actually negative. It can really be eye-opening, empowering, and confidence-building to see things you used to be embarrassed about in a new, positive light! Continue rereading your transformed statements to reflect on and truly digest them.

Highlighting What I'm Good At

Doing things that you are good at builds your confidence and self-esteem—two key components of self-love. Even if you have negative feelings about other aspects of your life, having something you know you're good at helps you feel more confident and capable. Then you are more likely to take on new challenges and achieve success.

How to Manage This

Be sure to recognize areas where you are strong. You may be a great listener or a fierce negotiator. Most of us spend far more time worrying about what we think are weaknesses than we do celebrating what we're good at. If that's true for you, this exercise can help you shift that balance to favor the positive.

Write It Out

For this activity, describe in detail three things you are good at by answering these questions about each one. These are things that you are confident in your ability to achieve.

FIRST THING I'M GOOD AT

How long did it take you to learn it?

What skills or personality traits helped you master it?

How do you feel when you are doing this activity?

Are there any ways you share your love for this activity with others?

SECOND THING I'M GOOD AT

How long did it take you to learn it?

What skills or personality traits helped you master it?

How do you feel when you are doing this activity?

Are there any ways you share your love for this activity with others?

THIRD THING I'M GOOD AT

How long did it take you to learn it?

What skills or personality traits helped you master it?

How do you feel when you are doing this activity?

Are there any ways you share your love for this activity with others?

Action Steps

This activity helps you recognize that you are good at more things than you realized. You should appreciate those areas of strength. Take in and feel good about those things. Let confidence and self-love arise from those positive feelings. Also, tap in to those feelings when you try to accomplish new things. You may not be as good at those at first, but feeling confident will help you believe in your ability to learn.

Savoring Happiness Wherever, Whenever!

We all experience so many different emotions every day. You probably wish some—like happiness—would stick around so you could savor those great feelings as long as possible! Unfortunately, in the hectic rush of our day-to-day lives, we often hurry our emotions on their way. While you want to accept and acknowledge *all* your feelings, this activity is about staying present and mindful during happy moments. Allowing yourself to fully enjoy happy times will boost feelings of self-love because you are putting yourself first. Prioritizing your happiness is a great way to show yourself that you deserve the best in life.

How to Manage This

One way to make happy feelings last longer and feel more powerful is to stay present and mindful of them. I practice mindfulness simply by taking a break, sitting by myself, and trying to push all my worries about the past and future out of my head. I think of a couple of great things that are going on in my life, and then I think about how thankful I am for them. You can try practicing mindfulness in this or lots of other ways too. It will help you focus on what's happening right now, in the present moment.

Write It Out

For this activity, sit alone in a comfortable place and take a few deep breaths in and out. Then complete the prompts here, focusing on the present as much as possible.

I am happy that I am:

I am happy that I was:

I am happy that I will:

I am happy that I can:

I am happy when:

I am grateful for:

I am grateful that:

I am grateful when:

I am grateful because:

When you've finished, reflect a bit. How did you feel when you were completing this activity? Did the answers come quickly, or did you have to think awhile? How does it feel to review what you wrote?

Action Steps

Your answers allowed you to connect with some positive things going on in your life. It's important to find moments for reflection and create space for gratitude—those are ways to practice more self-love. Try completing this exercise once a week. The more you do it, the easier it will become. Keep going! You'll start to notice and savor all the good things around you much more frequently—and it will encourage you to love all the parts of yourself.

Doing What's Right for Me

Basing your decisions on other people's opinions can lead to feelings of resentment, disappointment, and sometimes even depression. Being preoccupied with other people's perceptions of you tends to take away from your belief in and love of yourself. Don't let others determine how you feel about yourself or influence decisions that pertain to your life. Learn to trust your inner voice, acknowledge your gut feeling, and reflect on the power you have over your life. It is important to make sure that as you go through life, you're listening to your authentic voice.

How to Manage This

Part of practicing self-love is to believe in yourself and your ability to do what's best for you. A great way to make sure that you are listening to your authentic voice is by ensuring that you have protected or quiet time for yourself. You need time to ask yourself key questions about how you feel and what's important to you. It is helpful to have these reflection times to evaluate and refocus your energies on what is important for you.

Write It Out

For this activity, I want you to look back for a second. Write down a few things that you did not do in the past because you were afraid of someone else's judgment. After each one, write down what you'd do differently if you were not afraid.

Action Steps

Most times, when people worry what others will think, those opinions don't really have an effect on what is going on. Getting to a point where you don't care about others' opinions takes time. This activity may be the first step in achieving the goal of self-reliance. Review what you wrote periodically, especially when you begin to fall into old habits—your reflection might help boost your confidence to deal with future situations in a different way.

My Promises to Myself

Following through with tasks or opportunities is a great way to boost your confidence and strengthen the relationship that you have with yourself. When you finish what you set out to do, you should feel so proud of yourself and your abilities! The act of finishing is rewarding on its own, and that feeling is heightened when you take some time to reflect on the hard work and motivation that got you there. Savoring your victories is a great way to reinforce your faith in yourself and set you up for future successes as you accomplish more goals.

How to Manage This

A great way to ensure that you keep your promises is to remind yourself of the things that you said you were going to do. I like to put reminders in my phone so they're front of mind. Even goals like "Speak kindly to me" can be put in your phone to remind you.

Write It Out

Write down a few "promises to myself." Give five to seven examples of pledges you made to yourself, focusing on goals that help you promote self-love. For example, "I promise to start my day off verbally, stating aloud one thing that I'm proud of myself for doing."

1. ______________________________

____

2. ______________________________

____

3. ______________________________

____

4. ______________________________

____

5. ____

____

6. ____

____

7. ____

____

Now write your plan for how you intend to follow up with yourself and make sure to keep those promises. Do you need to enlist a friend to help keep you accountable? Write down your progress.

1. ____
2. ____
3. ____
4. ____
5. ____
6. ____
7. ____

Action Steps

The goal of this exercise is to work toward accountability. Keeping promises and following through are all measures of accountability. You want your word—the things you say to others *and* to yourself—to be meaningful and reliable. How good are you at keeping those promises? How are you making yourself accountable? Use the plan you created here to ensure that you follow up with yourself and begin a pattern of accountability that will last a lifetime. The pride you feel in yourself will be worth the effort.

Do I Need Help?

You—and everyone around you—are human beings. You will never get everything right; you will never be perfect. And that's okay! You are wonderful just as you are. Unfortunately, many of us get caught up in a perfection trap, where we want to do all things, all the time, all by ourselves. This is a recipe for burnout, exhaustion, failure—and a negative sense of self. Instead of loving yourself for all that you *are* doing, you focus on what's *not* being done or what's not top-notch. Luckily there's a solution for this scenario—asking for help!

How to Manage This

As you embrace your imperfection, it is helpful to recognize when you need help. Asking for help is a sign of your strength. It actually is to your benefit to identify when you need help. Understanding when it is time to ask for help may even prevent a more severe mental health crisis! Let go of the need to do everything yourself and accept a helping hand. I bet you don't mind helping out when a friend or loved one occasionally needs something—those people probably feel the same way about you.

Write It Out

Think about your weekly activities. Could any of them be completed by someone (or something) else, or in a way that makes it more efficient for you? Look at these examples for guidance. Then write down your own activities in the remaining spaces.

TASK	MAIN ISSUE WITH COMPLETING IT	HOW I COULD ASK FOR HELP
Grocery shopping	*The store I like is across town and it takes me a long time to get there after work.*	*Use that store's coupon for free grocery delivery.*
Taking my father to all his doctor's appointments.	*I am falling behind at work because I am taking a lot of time off.*	*See if my siblings could alternate appointments with me.*

TASK	MAIN ISSUE WITH COMPLETING IT	HOW I COULD ASK FOR HELP

Action Steps

Instead of automatically doing things as you've always done them, allow yourself to imagine a new reality where you're not as overwhelmed. Sometimes a small change can make a big difference in your workload or anxiety levels. This change will allow you to sustain your mental health without waiting for a crisis to occur. Remember, you deserve rest and relaxation. Treating yourself kindly by asking for help is a great way to show yourself love.

Self-Love from Those Who Love Me

As you journey toward practicing self-love, it can help to have an example of what loving yourself looks like. Friends and loved ones who treat you well are great models. Having people who love and believe in you can give you the strength to love yourself, grow, and evolve. Thinking about how and why others love and believe in you can help remind you of all the great things about yourself.

How to Manage This

While believing in yourself is the ultimate goal, outside validation can be important as well. Hearing that you're amazing from loved ones can build confidence and encourage you to notice these great things about yourself. Whenever I doubt myself, I love to find one person who knows me very well and ask them why they believe in me. Their words always give me the boost I need to keep going.

Write It Out

Use the following blanks to describe three people who believe in you.

_________________ *believes in me.* _________________ *shows me by*

____

____

_________________ *believes in me because* _________________

____

____

_________________ *supports me by* _________________

____

____

__________________ *believes in me.* __________________ *shows me by*

____

____

__________________ *believes in me because* ______________________

____

____

__________________ *supports me by* ______________________________

____

____

__________________ *believes in me.* __________________ *shows me by*

____

____

__________________ *believes in me because* ______________________

____

____

__________________ *supports me by* ______________________________

____

____

Action Steps

By writing down the various ways people believe in you, you can confirm that you have the support you need and remind yourself of all your good qualities. If you find it challenging to list several people who believe in you, consider using this exercise as a way to show gratitude to those who are there for you. You don't have to have a lot of supporters. One or two is fine. Although this is your journey, it does not have to be completed entirely alone. Let their kind words and actions be a model for how you should love yourself.

Fighting Off Impostor Syndrome

Impostor syndrome is feeling that you do not belong, you're not good enough for the position you are in, or you don't know what you're doing. We all have those doubts once in a while; that's normal. But if you're feeling like this every day, impostor syndrome could be negatively affecting your self-worth. You might feel inadequate, disappointed, or afraid that you'll be "caught." Impostor syndrome can also make you talk yourself out of opportunities that you are qualified for. Although you do have weaknesses, it is your strengths that got you exactly where you belong. Understand what your strengths are and how they work with your weaknesses to create the whole picture of yourself.

How to Manage This

Embracing both your flaws and your strengths as you grow can help ward off feelings of impostor syndrome. Loving myself—flaws and all—has been key to helping me maintain my confidence. If I happen to notice a flaw in myself, I am glad that I know about it because now I can work to correct it! But I also make sure to identify and acknowledge my strengths so that I see the whole picture, not just the negatives. Being you is what gave you all the opportunities in the first place. You are who you need to be in every moment.

Write It Out

In this activity, I want you to dive deep into assessing your flaws and strengths. First, write down three flaws or weaknesses you think you have. Maybe you're often running late, or you wish you spoke up more.

THINGS I CONSIDER MY WEAKNESSES

1. ______________________________

2. ______________________________

3. ______________________________

Now describe how you could potentially address those flaws.

Now write down five strengths you have. Maybe you're a reliable worker, a creative leader, or a great writer.

FIVE OF MY STRENGTHS

1. ______________________________

2. ______________________________

3. ______________________________

4. ______________________________

5. ______________________________

Action Steps

Look back over your lists. Take a moment to be proud of yourself for identifying the things you can improve as well as your strengths. Know that you always deserve love and success no matter what's on your lists. When natural feelings of self-doubt creep in, revisit your list of strengths to remind yourself of all you've got going for yourself.

Challenge Self-Limiting Beliefs

Self-limiting beliefs are negative thoughts that hold you back in some way. These negative thoughts can hinder your growth, devastate your sense of self-love, and sometimes even limit you physically. For example, you might not try out for a sports team because you think you'll never make it. Self-limiting thoughts can sound like "I don't have the right clothes to go to that party," or "I am not smart enough to apply for that job." This type of thinking can cause you to miss out on growth opportunities and fun outings and lead to disappointment, sadness, and self-doubt.

How to Manage This

Even though self-limiting beliefs might feel very powerful and true, you can gain control of these thoughts and change them. First, identify and isolate the limiting beliefs, then challenge them with positive declarations. This process will help you manage and reframe your thoughts and improve your mood. I've had to do this over time, and doing so has helped me practice more self-love. When these types of thoughts pop up—and believe me, it can happen to anyone—turn them around by stating something positive.

Write It Out

Sometimes we get in our own way, and believing these self-limiting thoughts is one way that happens. In the left-hand column, write down some self-limiting thoughts you've had this week. In the space next to each negative thought, write down an affirmation beginning with "I am...." An example is provided.

SELF-LIMITING BELIEF	ALTERNATE POSITIVE AFFIRMATION
I am not good enough for the team.	*I am a great addition to any team.*

SELF-LIMITING BELIEF	ALTERNATE POSITIVE AFFIRMATION

Action Steps

Listing your negative thoughts and countering them with positive affirmations will help you better manage these all-too-common self-limiting beliefs. Starting those affirmations with "I am" helps you center your thoughts and feelings, live in the present, and vocalize your inner power and self-love. We all have times when we doubt ourselves, but how you counteract those thoughts makes all the difference in the world. The next time you hear a self-limiting belief in your head, take a moment to reframe it in a positive way and see how your outlook improves!

CHAPTER 4
SADNESS

Unfortunately, sadness is an emotion all of us experience at various points in our lives. Whether the cause is a minor issue or grief that last months, it feels uncomfortable to deal with sadness. All your feelings are okay to feel, and you should allow yourself to recognize and acknowledge the pain you're experiencing. Hiding or denying your feelings will only allow them to fester and will make things harder for you down the road. In this chapter, you will learn more about the emotional layers of sadness, how to process your feelings, and some strategies for bouncing back when you're ready.

Feeling sad is a normal part of life. But if sadness dominates your life to the point where it affects your ability to work, maintain relationships, or function on a daily basis, that is a sign to reach out for professional help. A trained therapist can help you work through your feelings in a safe way.

Is It Sadness or Something Else?

Although it is unpleasant, feeling sadness is not a bad thing. Being able to feel sadness means that you are able to have a full emotional experience. Part of learning about sadness and depression is understanding that you *can* have one without the other. Having sadness for an extended period of time does not mean that you automatically have depression, but that is a good sign that it may be time to talk to a professional. Sadness that dominates your life can be a sign of depression.

How to Manage This

Whenever I feel sad, I like to explore those feelings and ask myself why I feel that way. I also try to determine if this mood is the primary emotion that I've been feeling for that day or that week. It's important to find out why you're feeling sad. And it's okay if you're not exactly sure why—sometimes the cause is not immediately clear or may include a few things together. That's where a professional can help.

Write It Out

In this activity, I want you to track your sad emotions for the next three weeks. If you noticed that you felt sad, write down exactly when the feelings arose, how they showed up, and why you might have felt sad. For example, maybe you felt sad on Tuesday morning on your way to work while listening to an audiobook, and you had to hold back tears. Once you've tracked your emotions, answer the reflection questions.

WEEK 1

DAY	WHEN?	HOW IT SHOWED UP	WHY?
Monday			

DAY	WHEN?	HOW IT SHOWED UP	WHY?
Tuesday			
Wednesday			
Thursday			
Friday			
Saturday			
Sunday			

WEEK 2

DAY	WHEN?	HOW IT SHOWED UP	WHY?
Monday			

DAY	WHEN?	HOW IT SHOWED UP	WHY?
Tuesday			
Wednesday			
Thursday			
Friday			
Saturday			
Sunday			

WEEK 3

DAY	WHEN?	HOW IT SHOWED UP	WHY?
Monday			
Tuesday			

DAY	WHEN?	HOW IT SHOWED UP	WHY?
Wednesday			
Thursday			
Friday			
Saturday			
Sunday			

REFLECTIONS:

- Are there certain days or times you feel sad?
- Did the same things cause sadness each time, or were the causes varied?
- Did the sadness impact your ability to carry on with your day?
- Did you notice any other patterns?

Action Steps

This activity gives you insight on when and why you're feeling sad. If you notice a pattern, there may be things you can do to feel less sad. For example, if you notice that you're extremely sad every Thursday after you watch a particular show, maybe it's a sign that that show might be a little emotionally overwhelming for you. It's also perfectly fine if you can't pinpoint a pattern. Remember, you should seek professional help when your sadness feels overwhelming or unwarranted and when you need an experienced guide to help you manage your feelings.

Depression 101

Depression appears in various ways. It can look like a loss of interest in activities that you used to enjoy. It can be a sad mood that lasts for days in addition to changes in your appetite, sleep, and so much more. Depression is one of the leading causes of disability worldwide. Disability means being unable to work or perform daily life functions. Being able to navigate depressive feelings and symptoms along with the help of your local and competent mental health professionals will be crucial in helping you maintain your mental health.

How to Manage This

Although depression can greatly impact your life, there is always hope! Seeking out and working with a mental health professional can be a true game changer in both the short and long term. And things you can do yourself, such as regular exercise and prioritizing sleep, can help to improve symptoms and maintain your mood.

Write It Out

In this activity, think about habits you notice about yourself when you're feeling low. When you're sad or stressed, do you tend to stay in bed longer? Do you sometimes avoid responsibilities? Do you leave texts from your friends unanswered? Write down anything that comes to mind.

Now that you've done that, be sure you are self-aware if you fall into any of those patterns. That might be a signal to check in with your therapist and get some help. Finally, write out some steps you could take to alleviate those low feelings. What can you do to help yourself when you aren't feeling your best? How can you work through your feelings? (Some activities in this book, such as How to Feel Difficult Feelings in Chapter 1, might help you.)

Action Steps

This activity serves as a snapshot of how you behave when your mental health isn't at its best. It will allow you to see how depression could manifest in your day and help you see signs that you need to dedicate time to improving your mental health. If responses didn't come easily to you, don't worry. That may be a sign that it's time to enlist the help of a professional. You'll find resources at the end of the book to help find the best mental health professional for you.

Shake Out of a Funk!

Everyone will have dips in their emotions sometimes—it is completely normal. What is important is learning how to deal with any periods of low mood to make sure that you get back to your best you. When you're in a bout of sadness, being able to bounce back will help you reclaim your happiness and get yourself back on track. When you return to being productive, you'll also likely boost your self-esteem. Feeling stuck in sadness could lead to such problems as depression, relationship difficulties, and low self-confidence. If you have trouble getting out of a prolonged period of sadness, it may be time to reach out for professional help.

How to Manage This

I like to embrace the moments when I'm in a funk. I got this idea from Brent Gleeson, a Navy SEAL who coined the phrase "Embrace the suck" and later shared it with an NFL team. He told the team to embrace the moments when they're in a funk and take a lesson from it. Leaning into the pain puts each team member in a better position to handle their frustrations, because something good is coming from it. This mindset helps the team as a whole and can help you avoid feeling frustrated by any low moods that arise. How can you embrace the suck?

Write It Out

For this activity, think about the last time you were in a funk. Maybe you were going through a rough breakup, or you just felt like you weren't where you wanted to be in life. Now that you're on the other side of the funk, think about ways that you embraced the suck. Did you learn something valuable from that breakup? Did you realize you wanted to start a new career?

If you're in a funk now, review what you did to embrace the suck in the past, and plan how you'll shake your current funk using this technique.

Action Steps

This activity will better prepare you to deal with the ups and downs that life brings. By embracing the suck of your personal lull, you're making a positive out of a negative. The plan you created now will help you envision a way out of this funk, so that you can come out a stronger and wiser person on the other side.

Overcoming Helplessness

One of the things that I often see in my patients who feel sad is a sense of helplessness. This sense of despair might come from being in a tough situation and having no confidence that you can get out of it. You might feel like there's no use in trying anything to improve your situation. When you experience this sort of despair, it impacts every aspect of your life because you feel unmotivated and lethargic.

How to Manage This

It's important to realize that you *are* able to equip yourself with the tools needed to bounce back from day-to-day feelings of helplessness. After I have a rough day, I like to sit back and think about ways that I was successful in turning that day around. Sometimes I will take my journal out and write down what I come up with—maybe one of my meetings was productive, or I was able to make a good dinner for myself. Keeping a journal is a useful tool for combating helplessness because you often forget all the little things you accomplish on any given day. Recording your successes can remind you that you can turn things around.

Write It Out

For this activity, think back to a rough day or a rough week you had recently. Describe what happened.

How did you handle what happened? What would you change about what you handled if it comes up again in the future? Write how you would handle it differently. (As you do this, give yourself some compassion and remind yourself that you were going through a rough time!)

Action Steps

This activity should give you the confidence to know that you are not helpless. You are capable and more than equipped to deal with the tough situations that life brings. When you notice yourself feeling helpless, return to this activity to remind yourself how you got out of the situation before. Update and add to your thoughts about how to handle feelings of helplessness so that you can refer to these ideas whenever you need them.

The Simple Things Matter

Sometimes sadness arises because your basic needs aren't being met. Things like eating enough, consuming a good variety of foods, and getting enough sleep seem boring and unimportant, but they are vital for mental health. Not only are they physical necessities, but they are also moments in your day that you should try to enjoy. When you are eating or sleeping poorly, you will feel run down and be quick to feel big emotions.

How to Manage This

Sadness can arise for lots of different reasons. If yours is due to basic needs not being met, you can improve your mood by taking care of those things. Making sure you're well rested and fed seems basic but can make a huge difference in your overall outlook. You'll feel more energetic, patient, and able to tackle your day.

Write It Out

You might not even know exactly what your basic needs look like. Take a few moments to think of what works best for your body, even if it's not what you're doing right now. For example, do you feel best after a small, light breakfast, or do you prefer a full, hearty plate of food? What is your bedtime goal?

Now let's identify *why* each of these things are important. This knowledge will help you stick to good habits because you know what benefits they bring you. For example, your quiet walk after dinner matters because it helps you digest and use up any leftover energy before bedtime. Your protein-packed breakfast matters because it gives you lasting energy to power through your busy mornings.

Action Steps

It probably felt good to reflect on the basic things that help set you up for mental health success. On tough days, just aim to do as many of the simple ones as you can. On days when you feel up to taking on more, try to do all of them. Your basic needs are the foundation on which you can rebuild your happiness.

Space to Be Human

You might be experiencing sad feelings because you are disappointed in yourself—perhaps too unfairly! We all judge ourselves for the experiences that we go through. Although some self-reflection can be useful, most of us instead nitpick and second-guess everything we say and do in a negative and unhelpful way. We do not give ourselves any grace to mess up and go through the setbacks that life comes with. We are all human. We will all fail at some point....And we have to accept that. Failing to accomplish something does not make *you* a failure—it gives you an opportunity to learn and be better.

How to Manage This

It's important to learn to accept failures as part of growing—as part of life. That's easier said than done, though. Even as a mental health professional, I might sometimes forget that I am human too. It's important to know that this feeling happens to everyone. Stepping back, taking an objective look, and viewing yourself and your experiences the same way you would for a good friend could make it easier for you to give yourself space to fail, process tough emotions, and come out feeling better.

Write It Out

For this activity, write down ways in which you believe you've failed yourself. For example, "I struck out at last week's softball game and feel like I cost my team the win," or "I feel like I did poorly in that interview for the job I really wanted." Write down any failures, past or present.

For the second part of this exercise, choose one example that really stings. Write out three alternative positive narratives, such as, "I still really enjoyed playing on my team, and no one on the team blames me for the loss," or "I learned a lot about job interviewing from that experience."

1. ____

____

____

2. ____

____

____

3. ____

____

____

Action Steps

I hope this activity helps you recognize that you are a human being, and it is okay to experience failure sometimes. It's natural to think about these failures from time to time, but if you continually berate yourself for any particular experience, one of your mental health goals should be to work through this self-judgment. Failures will happen, but they do not have to ruin your happiness or your health.

One Step Forward, Two Steps Back

Experiencing setbacks can make it hard to enjoy life and ward off sad feelings. Even though it's not a full failure, setbacks can temporarily derail your motivation and self-confidence. Maybe the next class you need to take is already full, or the place you wanted to rent is taken. Those obstacles won't prevent you from fulfilling your dreams of earning a degree or finding an apartment, but they will delay them a bit. That can lead to feelings of frustration, sadness, and disappointment.

How to Manage This

How do you typically deal with setbacks? Some of us charge ahead whereas others might give up altogether. The best approach may be somewhere in the middle of those two. I like to take a step back whenever I feel like I've encountered a situation that has stumped me. I remind myself that it is acceptable to take a break while I reassess the situation. Things may not always go just as you planned, but that is okay. Stepping back allows you to take a calm look at what is going on and brainstorm a solution.

Write It Out

For this activity, imagine that you are writing a letter to a friend who is going through a tough time that's very similar to the one you're experiencing. What would you say to this friend to help them overcome their setback? Write your letter here.

Action Steps

Chances are, the words you offered your friend were kind, hopeful, and compassionate. Reflecting on this activity can help you understand that it's normal to have setbacks and recognize that you can overcome them, which is probably just what you told your friend. Reread your kind words, try to internalize them, and apply the positivity and well-wishes to your own situation. Self-compassion is a great approach to mitigating sadness when you run into setbacks.

My Guide to "Blah" Days

Everyone has a "blah" day once in a while. You know how they look—nothing terrible happens, but nothing is particularly great either. You're a little tired, a little bored, or a little sad. How can you get through a day like this?

How to Manage This

There are three ways that you can manage a blah day. First, recognize that you don't have to be at your best every day. It's okay to have good and bad days. Next, understand that there's only so much that you can control. Focus on what you can control and let go of the rest. Lastly, learn to use those blah days to help you appreciate happier moments in life. When you can shift your focus to happier times, the blah days don't become overwhelming or turn into blah weeks.

Write It Out

Let's try to shift the focus of your blah day to happier times. List some happy thoughts, memories, and things you can keep front of mind when you're feeling a little sad.

HAPPY THOUGHTS	HAPPY MEMORIES	HAPPY THINGS
I am a smart person.	*That girls' night with my friends last Friday was a blast.*	*My dog*

HAPPY THOUGHTS	HAPPY MEMORIES	HAPPY THINGS

Action Steps

By making these lists, you will be able to position yourself to find happiness on the days when everything seems just blah. These simple things will help you realize that even on a day like that, there are bright spots that can make you feel better. They won't end blah days forever, but they will remind you of good moments to help get you through them.

The Overlap Between Depression and Burnout

Burnout is not technically the same as depression; however, the two conditions do share a lot of overlap in symptoms. For example, with both burnout and depression, you can experience a loss of interest in things that you used to enjoy, a hard time being productive at school or work, and isolation from family or friends. Burnout tends to be related to a lack of boundaries and specific situational factors, whereas the cause of depression may not be as easy to determine. It's important to reach out to a professional if you're feeling unsure of the cause of your sadness or feel that you need help.

How to Manage This

Even though burnout isn't the same as depression, it can also cause you to feel long periods of sadness. To tackle it, first determine the factors that are causing you stress. From there, you can create a solid plan to address those factors. This plan should include setting boundaries. Boundaries will help you avoid feeling burned out easily. It will also help you begin to prioritize rest. These methods can help you manage burnout and the sadness that goes with it.

Write It Out

In this activity, you'll write down recent times you were burned out. They could be from a specific work project, extra home responsibilities, or just the daily grind. Fill in the blanks to reflect on those times.

WHEN DID YOU FEEL BURNOUT?	WHY DO YOU THINK YOU FELT THAT WAY?	WHAT EMOTIONS DID YOU FEEL DURING THAT TIME?	HOW DID YOU (OR COULD YOU, NEXT TIME) MAKE YOURSELF FEEL LESS STRESSED?

WHEN DID YOU FEEL BURNOUT?	WHY DO YOU THINK YOU FELT THAT WAY?	WHAT EMOTIONS DID YOU FEEL DURING THAT TIME?	HOW DID YOU (OR COULD YOU, NEXT TIME) MAKE YOURSELF FEEL LESS STRESSED?

Action Steps

This exercise was designed to help you remember the feelings of burnout and understand what got you there so that you can recognize them sooner next time. Reviewing the *when*, *why*, and *how* of burnout will allow you to understand the importance of boundaries and position you to stand up for yourself better in the future. Remember, boundaries are completely healthy and help you and others understand your limits and learn to respect your time, needs, and space. For more ideas, see Setting Healthy Boundaries in Chapter 7.

How to Manage Mood Swings

Mood swings are normal. Everybody has them, and they are part of the human experience. One moment we're walking on cloud nine, and the next moment we're snippy—it's happened to all of us. This rollercoaster can sometimes make us feel uncomfortable, confused, or sad. Although you can't always stop mood swings, you can learn how to understand and manage them when they do happen.

How to Manage This

One effective way to manage mood swings is by giving yourself time between your thoughts and actions. Give yourself time to sit with your thoughts and begin to understand them before you do anything. Also, sometimes moodiness is attributed to feeling like you don't have control over things. Try to accept that you can't control everything. Lastly, make sure you're getting enough rest. Sometimes rest and relaxation can help you manage your moods. An important note: If mood swings begin to significantly alter the quality of your life, check in with a mental health professional to see if you need specific help.

Write It Out

In this activity, answer the following questions surrounding your mood swings. These will help you see the full picture of your life when you're experiencing mood swings.

What's making you upset?

What typically helps you feel better?

What does your day tend to look like when small things are irritating you?

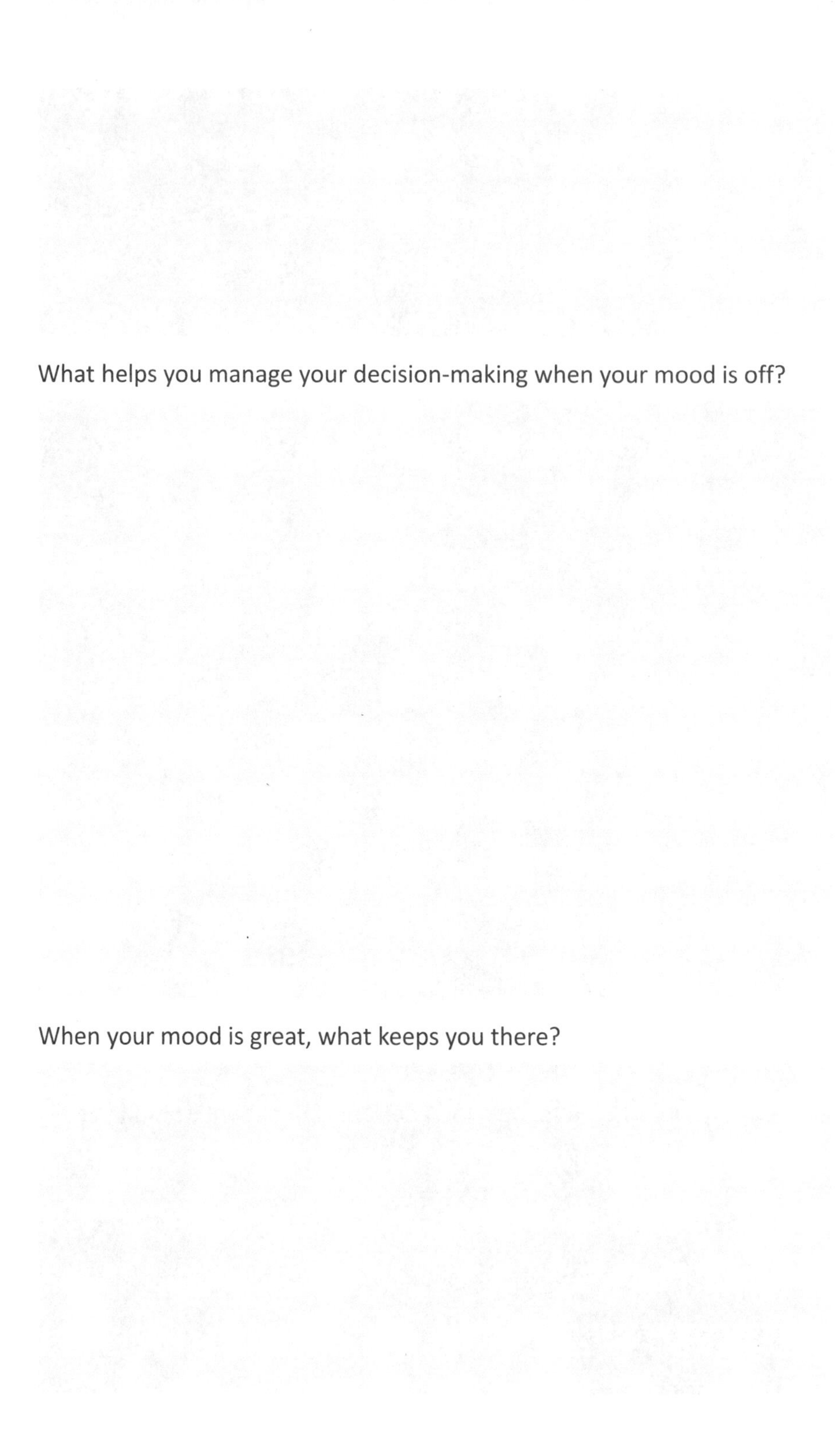

What helps you manage your decision-making when your mood is off?

When your mood is great, what keeps you there?

When your mood is great, what throws you off?

Action Steps

The goal of this activity is to help you determine how and when your mood impacts your life. Taking the time to think about your mood swings can help you become better aware when you are in those situations again. You can start to address, *in the moment*, any situations that you know could cause your mood to shift, instead of letting them linger and cause stress or sadness. For example, if you know you tend to get irritable when you miss your workout, you can prioritize that exercise to avoid a negative mood swing.

Don't Give Up Hope

Hope is a powerful thing. It can help you set goals, achieve growth, and imagine a wonderful future. A feeling of hopelessness is a potential sign of depression. That's something that mental health clinicians look for in their patients. Even if you're just feeling down and aren't depressed, it may be challenging to feel hopeful. It's important to try, though. Finding and maintaining a positive outlook for the future can help you ward off long-term sadness, low self-confidence, and lack of motivation.

How to Manage This

Journaling about your feelings, leaving upbeat messages of hope in your phone, or writing sticky notes with affirmations can help you refocus on a positive future. I always like to tell my patients who are struggling with hopelessness to at least be curious enough to stick around and see what tomorrow brings. A good overall way to manage hopelessness is by focusing on things you enjoy and are curious about. Be future-oriented. Thinking about possibilities can help alter your outlook and restore your hope.

Write It Out

List some things you're looking forward to, including the why and how. These can vary from a new job to a new addition to the family.

I'M LOOKING FORWARD TO	WHY?	HOW DOES IT MAKE ME FEEL?

I'M LOOKING FORWARD TO	WHY?	HOW DOES IT MAKE ME FEEL?

Action Steps

This activity will serve as a reminder of the things that make you hopeful. When you're feeling overwhelmed or down, it is easy to focus on negative things. Hopelessness can happen when you forget about possibilities. Thinking about things you're looking forward to, why, and how they make you feel are important steps to helping you get back on track mentally.

Grounding Myself in Gratitude

When you experience feelings of sadness, you can place yourself in a more positive mental space just by showing gratitude for all the good things in your life. When you are grateful, you center yourself in the present and think about things that you are appreciative of. This makes it very difficult to be anxious because anxiety cannot live in the present—it is usually related to a past event or a future worry. Gratitude also has a way of making you feel better about yourself and your situation.

How to Manage This

Center yourself in the present and consider all the things you can be grateful for. I love to think about something that my grandmother used to do for me growing up. She would sing this song about counting your blessings, and after that, she would ask my siblings and me to talk about the things that we were grateful for. It was a good way to teach us about gratitude. You can create more gratitude in your life by vocalizing your appreciation every day. Set an alarm for each evening to go over your day, and write down (or say) what you're grateful for that day.

Write It Out

In this activity, you will track your gratitude for a week. You can list more than one thing on each day.

DAY	WHAT ARE YOU GRATEFUL FOR TODAY?	HOW DID YOU SHOW YOUR GRATITUDE?
Monday		
Tuesday		

DAY	WHAT ARE YOU GRATEFUL FOR TODAY?	HOW DID YOU SHOW YOUR GRATITUDE?
Wednesday		
Thursday		
Friday		
Saturday		
Sunday		

Action Steps

The goal of this activity is to serve as a reminder of all the things for which you are grateful. It is all too easy to overlook your fortunes most of the time, but feeling gratitude can help you ward off sadness. Practice reflecting on gratitude daily to lift your spirits and remind yourself of happiness. Revisit this list when you need to remember all that you have.

Celebrating My Wins

How often do you stop, recognize your accomplishments, and take time to celebrate what you have done? Most people forget to do that—a cycle we need to change. Self-reflection and realization are important to a healthy view of yourself and can help you overcome normal periods of sadness. By allowing yourself to pause and realize all the amazing things that you've done, you will boost your self-esteem and maintain the confidence needed to do amazing things in the future. It all starts with taking time to appreciate yourself.

How to Manage This

I like to work hard, but I've learned to take a break now and then to appreciate my accomplishments, big or small. (I also pause to look at others' accomplishments—it spreads good vibes when you acknowledge those around you and celebrate their wins too!) It's important to reflect on how far you've come and savor each accomplishment.

Write It Out

Take some time to think about your recent accomplishments. Did you graduate from a school or college? Were you ever on the honor roll or named employee of the month? Don't forget to look beyond traditional accomplishments. Did you finish a hard video game? Nothing is too small to celebrate if it matters to you! List some of your accomplishments and how you achieved them in the space here.

ACCOMPLISHMENT	HOW I ACHIEVED IT

ACCOMPLISHMENT	HOW I ACHIEVED IT

Action Steps

Revise your list periodically and add to it as you work through new tasks. Once a month, stop and remember the *how* and *why* of your accomplishments. This process should help you recognize how observing and appreciating your accomplishments can make you feel more determined to achieve your next goal. Focusing on your past victories and setting goals for future success can keep sad feelings at bay or help you overcome them when they appear.

CHAPTER 5

STRESS AND ANXIETY

Stress and anxiety are all too common in today's society. Whether it's small-picture stress (like worrying that you'll be late for a meeting) or big-picture anxiety (like waiting for a medical diagnosis), we all deal with stress daily. Our bodies have both physical and mental reactions to stress. Physically, we might experience muscle tension, fatigue, insomnia, and high blood pressure. Mentally, we might experience apathy, an inability to focus, and moodiness or irritability.

Although you can't eliminate all stressors from your life, you can learn to identify and manage them in a healthy way. In this chapter, we will look at stress and discover why it is not always a negative thing. You will also learn about stress signals that can tell you that you need to recalibrate something in your life. By the end of this chapter, you'll begin to recognize that managing stress goes hand in hand with managing positive mental health.

Uncertainty Is Okay!

One common cause of stress is dealing with uncertainty in some form—what job you'll land, whether your relationship will move to the next level, or if a cause you believe in will advance forward. Uncertainty is a natural part of life and doesn't automatically have a negative impact on your mental health. However, your response to uncertainty can significantly affect your mental health. Think about how you respond to an unknown in your life. Do you find yourself unable to sleep as your mind races? Unable to focus because your thoughts always return to this uncertain situation? These reactions can quickly impact your everyday life if you don't get a handle on them.

How to Manage This

One effective way to face uncertainty is to truly accept that you can't control the future. It sounds simple, but it's not that easy to do. When you can release that connection, though, it's truly liberating. You may disagree or see lack of control as a challenge to your need for order. A good way to manage that urge for control is to learn to be more adaptable. Adaptability can help you handle some anxiety associated with uncertainty. It's important for you to try to lean into the unknown, to accept the future as an exciting next step.

Write It Out

In this activity, you are going to examine uncertainty in your life. Think of things that you have to deal with but do not have full control over. Write at least three of these things down. After each statement, write how it makes you feel to deal with this uncertainty.

Now brainstorm how you can alleviate your sense of worry over these things. The way that you alleviate worry depends on you as a person or the particular situation. You know yourself best, so take some time to detail how you can help yourself embrace things you have control over and let go of worry about what you can't change. For example, I once had a friend who was about to go into surgery. I couldn't control how the surgery would go, but I could offer him support and friendship at that difficult time. Directing my energy in that positive way helped lessen some of my anxiety.

Action Steps

This activity will get you to take a close look at the things that you cannot control and encourage you to identify and process the uncomfortable feelings that come with being uncertain about the future. It is my hope that as you practice doing this, you will become better at letting go of trying to control everything. You *can't* control certain things, and the unknown *can* be scary. However, fear or anxiety won't stop uncertainty from coming. Shifting your focus to areas within your control will help you regain some power in the situation.

Understanding Anxiety

Anxiety is a normal and common emotion, but this emotion in excess can be characterized as a mental health condition. With anxiety, an individual may have a consistent feeling of dread or may spend a lot of their time worrying about the future. Similarly, stress is an individual's reaction to a certain situation or a threat. As stress builds up, an individual is likely to experience feelings of anxiety. But, if your anxiety gets the point where you have a diagnosis, it is helpful to know that anxiety disorders are among the most common mental health conditions. Many people struggle with similar issues, so don't lose hope—you can do a lot to manage your symptoms.

How to Manage This

I tell my patients that anxiety is almost an exaggerated fear of the future. One simple way to combat anxiety is to stay in the present. Practicing mindfulness and gratitude helps you bring your focus back to the present—where anxiety cannot exist—as opposed to being in the future—where anxiety dominates. (Check out Grounding Myself in Gratitude in Chapter 4 for ideas on practicing gratitude.)

Write It Out

Let's take a deep dive into your emotions. Use the following chart to answer questions about your top anxieties.

WHAT MAKES ME ANXIOUS?	WHY?	WHAT HELPS ME TO COME BACK TO THE PRESENT MOMENT?	HOW DO I FEEL ONCE I "COME BACK"?

WHAT MAKES ME ANXIOUS?	WHY?	WHAT HELPS ME TO COME BACK TO THE PRESENT MOMENT?	HOW DO I FEEL ONCE I "COME BACK"?

Action Steps

This activity helps you to develop a better understanding of what's causing your anxiety and how you manage it. Becoming aware that your anxiety typically exists in the future, not the present, can be very liberating. Use the activity chart again and again in times when you're feeling anxious to identify the root of your anxiety and the ways that work for you to overcome it.

What Can I Control?

Like uncertainty, feelings of helplessness can cause stress and anxiety or make them worse. Recognizing the things that you have control over helps combat feelings of helplessness. Just like hopelessness, helplessness is a common emotion in individuals who struggle with depression. However, hopelessness is a state of mind in which a person questions what they have to live for. Helplessness is a state of mind in which you feel powerless and doubt whether you have the ability to overcome a situation, so you might give up before you even try. Both might take time to overcome, but understanding areas within your control can help.

How to Manage This

I always tell my patients, "You are in the driver's seat, and I'm riding shotgun with you." This statement allows my patients to feel empowered and helps them recognize that they are in control of their lives; they are the ones who can make the necessary changes needed to get them where they want to go. Feeling empowered has to do with feeling in control. You can manage feelings of helplessness by focusing on areas you can control instead of dwelling on things out of your control.

Write It Out

Inside the circle, jot down things you can control. These could include the times you go to bed and wake up, the people you choose to spend time with, and the things you consume— in various ways (for example, what you eat or information you get from the news or social media). Outside the circle, list the things you cannot completely control, such as the weather or the economy.

THINGS YOU CAN CONTROL

THINGS YOU CANNOT CONTROL

Action Steps

This exercise aims to help you remember that you may not feel like you are in control every day, but you are. I bet you found many more things to write inside your circle than outside of it! Focus your attention on what you wrote inside the circle—where you have the power to reevaluate, change, or adjust your plans. Use the visual reminder that things you wrote *outside* the circle are also *outside* your control. Even if you wrote a few things outside your circle, you are not helpless to create change in your life because there are plenty of things inside the circle to work on. You are more than capable of living a life you are proud of—a life where you feel loved, respected, and worthy.

Find the Silver Linings

Some stressful situations offer an opportunity in disguise. Learning how to find the silver lining is a superpower because it helps you reframe situations by looking for positive aspects. This way, you can recognize when an opportunity comes your way. This may translate into a chance to advance at work, take time to relax, or receive help.

How to Manage This

Managing how you look at life takes practice. If you're prone to thinking negatively, it helps to write down and repeat affirmations. You can also take time to reminisce about how you somehow got through some hard times; it is useful to remember that things tend to work out. Lastly, consider how you react to others' opinions. Try not to be bothered about what others think of you or your choices. This reminder can really help you avoid the pitfalls of negative thinking and feeling like you're not where you're "supposed" to be. An important note: If you have certain mental health conditions, it can be extremely challenging to think positively, but a professional can help you.

Write It Out

For this activity, write about the last time that you were stuck in a situation where you felt anxious, but it actually turned out well for you. Describe the situation in as much detail as possible.

Now reflect on the situation, what went well, and what you could do differently next time. Document any events or actions that you did but maybe didn't realize at the time. Try to understand how those helped cause your success.

Now describe how it felt to no longer have to worry about the issue when it was over. Perhaps you were worrying about something that didn't end up happening. Were you perhaps worrying unnecessarily? Write about that too. Finally, note if any unexpected opportunities came from this situation.

Action Steps

Recognizing that you have dealt with similar situations, and had success in them, can help combat feelings of anxiety when new situations arise. The next time you find yourself focusing on the negative when you're stressed out, see where you have room for improvement. Also, try to be aware of any tendencies you may have to overly worry, and remind yourself that some stressful situations could create unexpected opportunities!

What Am I Afraid Of?

In general, being fearful is not a bad thing. However, sometimes we use our fear as a disguise for other feelings we have. These hidden feelings may range from insecurity to anxiety. The fear created from these feelings can be detrimental to your progress toward good mental health, as well as any of your other goals. You might be afraid of failing or stepping out on your own. These fears can hold you back from achieving your goals, which causes lower self-confidence, frustration, and disappointment.

How to Manage This

It is important to stare your fears directly in the face. When staring them down, you let your fears know that you are capable of managing them. This may be a cliché, but you can do anything you set your mind to. Say aloud or to yourself that this particular fear will not hold you back. The more you do this, the more empowered and confident you feel, and the easier it becomes to handle the obstacles that might cause a sense of fear in you.

Write It Out

In this activity, we will look at how you plan to overcome fear. Write down the things you're fearful of. In the right-hand column, write down how you plan to overcome the fears.

MY FEAR	HOW DO I ACT WHEN I'M AFRAID OF THIS THING?	HOW CAN I OVERCOME THOSE FEARS?

MY FEAR	HOW DO I ACT WHEN I'M AFRAID OF THIS THING?	HOW CAN I OVERCOME THOSE FEARS?

Action Steps

This activity helped you identify your fears, recognize how you react to them, and envision a plan to tackle them. Fear is part of life. There's nothing wrong with feeling fearful, but your goal should be to try to push past it. Remembering that you *can* overcome fear is something you must do as part of your journey. Like a lot of other things, the more you do it, the easier it will become.

Self-Awareness FTW

Being self-aware refers to having an understanding of what you do and why you do it. It may seem like everyone has that—but it's actually easy to go about your day without stopping to check in with yourself about what you're feeling and why. (Refer to Checking In on Myself in Chapter 1 for more information on how to do that.) The key is to have the right amount of self-awareness. Having too much self-awareness could actually increase anxiety. Let me explain. Sometimes when people realize that they have issues that need to be fixed, they experience sadness, frustration, helplessness, or low self-confidence. This happens more often if they realize that there's an issue but don't know how to deal with it. You want to use self-awareness as a tool to help you grow, not put yourself down.

How to Manage This

I am a big fan of being kind to yourself. You may uncover some habits that you could improve as you work on your mental health, but don't make yourself feel bad about them. As you learn more about yourself, it's important to recognize that when you made mistakes in the past, you were doing the best you could with information you had at that moment. Now that you know more and you're using this mental health workbook, I believe that you are in a position to do better.

Write It Out

Write down some things that you've learned about yourself so far as you've read this book. Then write down one small improvement you can make for each topic.

THING I'VE LEARNED ABOUT MYSELF	HOW I COULD IMPROVE IT

THING I'VE LEARNED ABOUT MYSELF	HOW I COULD IMPROVE IT

Finally, I want you to write the following phrase in this space: "I am in control of my life, and I am able to make small improvements that can make a big difference!" This statement will help remind you that your self-awareness should be used in positive ways.

Action Steps

You learn a lot about yourself while trying to improve your mental health. It's important to write those things down and reflect on where you've been and where you plan on going. This record will serve as a reminder that even though you have areas you want to improve, you are still doing a very good job and should be proud of that. Continue to use your self-awareness as a tool for growth, not to add to your anxiety and stress levels.

Ditch Social Anxiety

Social anxiety is an anxiety disorder that manifests itself as an intense fear of certain social situations. Social anxiety is very sneaky, and it's also very silent. A lot of times people may not realize that they suffer from social anxiety until there's some type of consequence or impairment that happens within their life, which makes them question why they act the way that they do in certain public settings. Social anxiety can be very stressful and unpleasant, but there are ways to address this issue, whether or not you have an official diagnosis.

How to Manage This

For some people, practicing social interactions can help alleviate the stress that comes with them. One easy way to start a conversation is to compliment someone. By giving people simple compliments, you make them feel better about themselves and open yourself up to the likelihood of having a positive conversation. This opening can help you become more comfortable in social settings as you realize that there are many parts of yourself that people enjoy and you are a pleasure to be around.

Write It Out

Imagine that you are out in public and face-to-face with an acquaintance from your community, or a stranger. Write down a few compliments you could share with the person. An example is shown. This is a form of preparing to be more comfortable in social situations. Being kind and honest are great guides for compliments. Stay away from compliments about someone's body, as that could make the person uncomfortable.

PERSON	COMPLIMENT	FEELING
Neighbor	*Nice flower bed, love the new door paint, cute dog*	*It feels really good to make my neighbor smile.*

PERSON	COMPLIMENT	FEELING

Action Steps

The goal of this exercise is to try to become more comfortable speaking to people you don't know well. Imagining the situation or the meeting before it happens should help you feel more prepared for the real-life encounter. If you already have some potential words in your head, you might not feel so anxious trying to think of something to say. As with everything, it takes practice. If you are nervous about meeting new people, repeat and revisit this exercise to help you feel more comfortable. If you find these ideas too daunting to even try, you might benefit from meeting with a professional.

It's Not the End of the World

Much of what we worry and stress about doesn't actually come to pass. This is especially true when you imagine an awful worst-case scenario. Instead of considering what's most likely to happen, your mind may go to some terrible place where everything seems bleak. The trouble with this kind of thinking is that it drains you physically and mentally, and it's a waste of your precious time and energy.

How to Manage This

In my practice, I've seen a lot of what's called *catastrophic thinking*: someone's mind automatically defaults to the worst possible result without acknowledging that things could be a little bit better—or even much better. To combat catastrophic thinking, it's helpful to expand your mind to the potential positive possibilities. This mental expansion can help you live life with a bolder approach.

Write It Out

In this activity, you'll see how infrequently a catastrophic worst-case scenario happens. Write down two times when you were so worried something terrible would happen. Then write down what *actually* happened.

SCENARIO 1

What I Thought Would Happen

What Actually Happened

SCENARIO 2

What I Thought Would Happen

What Actually Happened

Action Steps

When you review what you wrote, did you find that a lot of your worry was unfounded? Next time, try saving your precious time, sleep, and energy. Say to yourself, "I can sense my mind racing with all those awful potential scenarios. None of them is likely to happen. I'm better off focusing on the middle ground, which is probably what will take place."

Don't Sweat Changes

Change is a common cause of anxiety, regardless of your age or situation. Whether you're a toddler entering a new childcare facility or an adult starting a new job, change can be scary! It sometimes causes feelings of inadequacy, self-doubt, or fear. Being resistant to change makes those feelings even worse. Resisting may also keep you from having new and valuable experiences that will help you grow and achieve your goals. Change happens all the time, and I'm here to tell you that being able to adjust to changes as they come is a superpower. Being adaptable and willing to accept change and new things can greatly benefit you and enlighten your experiences.

How to Manage This

A great way to handle the changes that life throws at you is to try to adopt a mindset that you can handle change. This mental shift doesn't mean change will be easy to accept or always good, but it puts you in a strong and positive place to deal with the change. The ups and downs of life happen, but it's up to you to manage them by facing them with confidence and optimism.

Write It Out

Think about some major life changes you've gone through. Write them in the spaces here. Then, answer the prompts to take a deeper look into why you felt resistant, whether or not your worries were well-founded (a lot of times they're not!), and plan how to react more positively in the future.

LIFE CHANGE	WHY WAS I RESISTANT TO THIS CHANGE?	DID YOUR FEARS COME TO PASS?	HOW CAN I REACT IN A MORE POSITIVE WAY IN THE FUTURE?

LIFE CHANGE	WHY WAS I RESISTANT TO THIS CHANGE?	DID YOUR FEARS COME TO PASS?	HOW CAN I REACT IN A MORE POSITIVE WAY IN THE FUTURE?

Action Steps

Considering the major changes in your life may bring up mixed emotions. It's important to recognize those feelings as the *why* of your resistance to that change. Because those worries often end up not being an issue, it's a good idea to note when those worries were unfounded so you can try to avoid unnecessary stress in the future. Your goal is to work through feelings and discover why some feelings hold you back or hinder your experiences. Finally, developing a plan for working *with* change, instead of against it, will help you navigate the next time life throws a curveball in your direction.

Take Things As They Come

A lot of times we get ahead of ourselves as life is happening—always looking ahead to the next thing instead of enjoying what we've just achieved. However, by operating in the present and taking things as they come, you can avoid being anxious about what's still to come. Remember, anxiety doesn't really operate in the present. Live in the present moment, accepting what's around you right now, and you're more likely to find peace and gratitude.

How to Manage This

One way that I encourage my patients to take things as they come is through a concept called *radical acceptance*. This means that when great things happen, you allow yourself to recognize that greatness has happened; you see the event for exactly what it is. You don't immediately turn to the next thing, or imagine some other scenario that could happen as a result of this event. You simply accept it and process it right now. Of course, when bad things happen, you also need to see them for exactly what they are as well. Radical acceptance allows you to go through any feelings and then begin to heal as necessary.

Write It Out

Write down two things that you are happy about in your life right now, and two things that you are not as happy about.

TWO THINGS I'M HAPPY ABOUT

1. ______________________________

____

____

2. ______________________________

____

____

TWO THINGS I'M NOT HAPPY ABOUT

1. ______________________________

____

____

2. ______________________________

____

____

Now I want you to write the following phrase: "I fully accept that these things are happening right now, and I will allow myself to go through the necessary emotions required to be fully present in this moment." Taking the time to write these words can allow you the time and space to process your feelings about each event.

Action Steps

These reflections can help you recognize and process your feelings. Becoming more aware of your feelings in the moment allows you to face and accept them. All feelings are trying to tell you something, so don't be afraid to acknowledge whatever arises. Practice and revisit this exercise to help you become more aware in the moment. It is my hope that this activity will allow you to operate more within the present and to allow things to happen naturally for you.

CHAPTER 6
CONFIDENCE

We've already talked a lot about confidence in this book—and with good reason. Confidence is an important part of your mental health journey because it provides the strong foundation that allows you to tackle problems big and small, short- and long-term. When you feel good about yourself and your abilities, you're more likely to take on challenges, achieve your goals, and feel happy. Conversely, when you are insecure or unsure of yourself, you unknowingly slow down your progress and self-sabotage.

This chapter focuses on ways to build confidence and value your most authentic self. Being able to lean into your most authentic self and tap in to your inner confidence will enable you to reach new heights! Confidence is one of the building blocks to better mental health, stronger relationships, more mindful self-care, and more self-awareness. Many of us struggle to find confidence, but the simple exercises in this chapter will help you practice this skill little by little.

Hyping Myself Up

Have you ever watched an athlete prepare for a big event? They may jump repeatedly, talk to themselves, listen to music, or do something else. They are hyping themselves up. Learning how to hype yourself up is a fun way to build self-confidence and mental fortitude. You will not always have part of a support system by your side, or a cheerleader right there when needed. Hyping yourself up is just another way to build self-reliance—an important step in bettering your mental awareness.

How to Manage This

A great way to start is to figure out what makes you energized. Is it certain songs? A particular stretch or warmup exercise? Reading inspirational quotes? What helps you recognize your strengths, believe in your ability to make things happen, and conquer obstacles? Over time, you will react immediately to these things and then you can lean into this hyped-up version of yourself!

Write It Out

In the list here, check the ways you can hype yourself up. Some of these may be outside your comfort zone, but consider trying them just to change things up! Add any of your own ideas in the spaces provided.

- ❑ Sing along to my favorite rap song
- ❑ Jump up and down
- ❑ Look in the mirror and tell myself how awesome I am
- ❑ Create a positive chant
- ❑ Eat my favorite food
- ❑ Write an affirmation
- ❑ Watch my favorite TV show
- ❑ Talk to a loved one on the phone
- ❑ ____________________
- ❑ ____________________
- ❑ ____________________
- ❑ ____________________
- ❑ ____________________

Now that you've written those down, try one now and write down how that made you feel.

Try a different "hype method" before your next three events when you need some energy and confidence. Write down how each made you feel.

EVENT 1

EVENT 2

EVENT 3

Action Steps

Let's face it: For many of us, it is easier and faster to point out all the ways we *don't* measure up instead of all the ways we are awesome. Luckily, you can learn to count on yourself for motivation and appreciation. Practice telling yourself how awesome you are and how great your accomplishments are. It may feel odd at first, but becoming your own "hype person" will help you create a lasting habit that is positive and effective.

Me at My Best Looks Like...

It's important to recognize what your best self is, so that you'll know when things feel different. Your body will send you signs that something is wrong, but you may not recognize them if you don't know what your best—your "doing well"—is. Everyone's best self will look different. You might feel calm and relaxed, but someone else might feel full of energy and upbeat. This is all part of really getting to know yourself. Knowing what your "best" looks like will help you become more proactive in your self-care.

How to Manage This

When you picture your best self, what does it look, sound, and feel like? Taking time to understand "your best" is important. It will help you recognize traits and actions that you affiliate with feeling good. This method is also helpful for managing your day-to-day feelings and better recognizing when things feel off. When you check in on yourself and find that you're not at your best, you can take steps to address what's not right.

Write It Out

In the space here, describe the last time that you felt at peace or content. Try to be very specific in your description, and bring in as many senses as you can. Where were you? What sights, sounds, or smells were you experiencing? What did your body feel like? What did your voice sound like?

Action Steps

It may be challenging to fully describe your best. We often get in the habit of just going through the emotions—pushing through when we don't really feel our best. However, this activity will help you review the feelings and senses associated with feeling your best. This is a unique description that only you can provide. The goal is for you to slowly begin recognizing signs that your body or mental state has changed. Becoming more in tune with your needs will improve your self-care and help you get back to your best.

Defining Confidence

Understanding what confidence means to you encourages you to listen to your voice and move forward with purpose. If you've struggled with building confidence in the past, it's important to take small steps in discovering what confidence looks like to you. However, once you understand and build confidence, you'll feel more capable and in control.

How to Manage This

Defining confidence can be challenging, but this activity will help you. You have to understand the role confidence plays in your life and relationships, and then find your way to establish that strong sense of self in your daily routines. If you aren't sure where to start, observe individuals you deem to be confident. Which of their habits resonates with you? Could you mirror any of them in your own life?

Write It Out

For this activity, think about what confidence means to you. Answer the following prompts:

Confidence means...

I believe this because...

I'd like to be more confident so that...

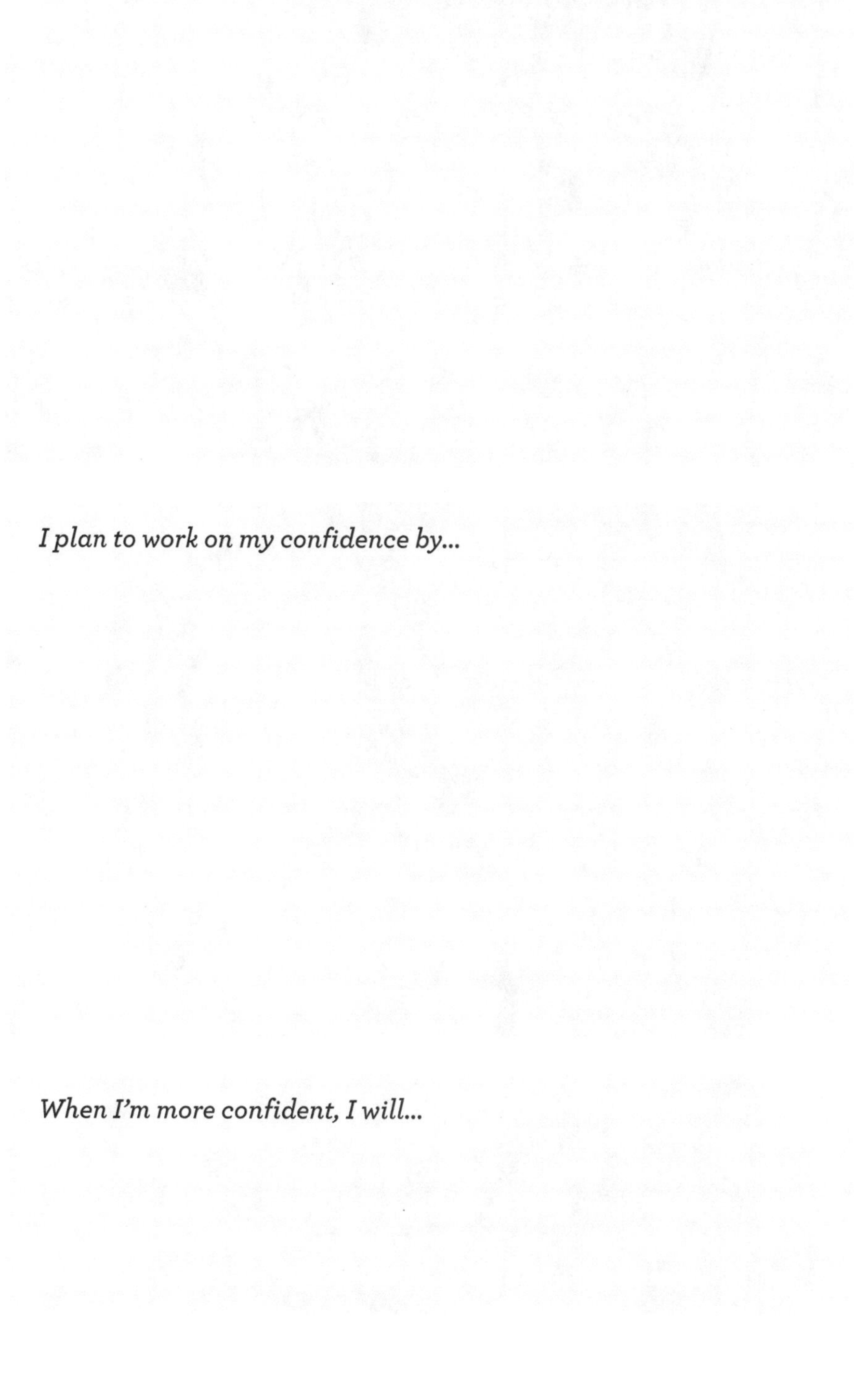

I have not been confident in the past because...

I plan to work on my confidence by...

When I'm more confident, I will...

Once I accomplish that, I will...

Action Steps

The goal of this activity is to help you discover your feelings surrounding confidence and work toward becoming more confident. After answering the prompts, reflect on how you feel about each answer. Focus on improving each day through the ideas you wrote. Consider using some of your responses as affirmations you can say in front of a mirror or write on sticky notes to hang in places you'll see frequently. By creating ways to improve your way of thinking, you are well on your way to becoming more confident.

Try New Things

A lack of confidence sometimes discourages us from trying new things. If you're too hesitant to tackle something new, you're staying in the same place—which is the opposite of the growing and learning you probably hope to do in your life. Alternatively, trying new things—even if you're not immediately successful at them—will show you that you are capable of learning new skills and improving yourself.

How to Manage This

Trying new things isn't easy if you haven't done that in a while. To start, try small, relatively easy activities that can quickly boost your confidence. For example, you could try the next level of something you already do well—such as taking on a small extra project at work, cooking a different version of a favorite recipe, or coaching a team in a sport you excel at. When you look back at a situation you just conquered, consider why you thought it was difficult before you attempted it. Remember that every bit of progress is a step in the right direction.

Write It Out

Are there some things you wish you could do? In this exercise, you're going to change those *I wishes* into *I cans*! Write down what you wish you could do. Then explain exactly why you think you can't do it. Next, cross out that "reason" and instead write down why that wish could actually come true. For example, you might write, "I wish I could become a nurse. ~~I think I can't because school is too expensive.~~ I can because I can look for financial aid to help pay."

I wish I could ____

____

I think I can't because __________________________________

____

I can because ____

____

I wish I could ____

____

I think I can't because ____

____

I can because ____

____

I wish I could ____

____

I think I can't because ____

____

I can because ____

____

Action Steps

This process will help you believe in your capabilities. It's important to work your way out of a doubting mindset in which you're afraid to tackle anything new. You're capable of trying new things and discovering new interests. You'll succeed many times and fail others—both of which are a part of life. When you find yourself slipping into *I wish*-type statements, redo this exercise to put yourself in a can-do, action-oriented frame of mind.

I'm a Little Rock Star

You've probably heard that everyone is special since grade school. Well, it's true—there is no one exactly like you. Being able to recognize that we all have different strengths is a huge superpower. Recognizing your specialness will allow you to be more confident in your abilities so that you can go out and accomplish the things that you want to do.

How to Manage This

A simple way to figure out what makes you special is to ask people close to you the following question, "What is something that I am very good that people usually struggle with?" You can also look through past accomplishments and find things that made you stand apart from your peers. It's important to ensure that your feelings about yourself are positive. By finding ways that showcase your unique style, you'll soon develop more confidence to feel like a rock star!

Write It Out

Call or text five people and ask them, "What are two things I am very good at?" Write down their responses in the space here. Did more than one person give the same answer? Do you agree? What I love the most about this exercise is that you can do it on two different days and call a different set of people each time and get brand new responses!

Action Steps

Now that you've completed the activity, did you notice anything interesting about the responses? Consider how other people see you and how you see yourself. There will be days that you don't feel like a rock star; that's normal. During those days, come back to this activity to review the kind or interesting responses from those closest to you. You'll soon remember that you are worthy and unique.

The Unusual Things I Love about Myself

Being different can sometimes be isolating. Maybe you have a learning difference that makes things more challenging for you. Maybe something you love about your appearance is outside society's norms. Maybe your peers don't consider your interests "cool." We all have something different about us, but some differences are more challenging than others. That's why it's important to learn how to work *with* your differences instead of against them. Accepting who you are and moving forward in a positive way will help you believe in yourself, trust your gut, and feel confident in your decisions.

How to Manage This

What unique things do you love about yourself? When you answer, don't consider society's messages or other people's judgments. Focus on what makes you feel happy, fulfilled, and like your best self. Once you recognize these things, you can work on accepting them and loving yourself just as you are. You can also focus on your unique strengths and build confidence from them.

Write It Out

Think about all that makes you unique. Write down seven unique traits and seven unique abilities. How are they unique? What makes them different?

SEVEN UNIQUE TRAITS

1. ______________________________

2. ______________________________

3. ______________________________

4. ______________________________

5. ______________________________

6. ____________________

7. ____________________

SEVEN UNIQUE ABILITIES

1. ____________________

2. ____________________

3. ____________________

4. ____________________

5. ____________________

6. ____________________

7. ____________________

Action Steps

The goal of this exercise is for you to understand that there are many amazing things about yourself that you should celebrate. Focusing on your unique traits, abilities, and looks will help you develop more self-confidence, pride, and joy. Review your list from time to time to remember just how unique and needed you are.

Building Confidence

Building confidence sounds simple but takes time and effort. It's very similar to building a new house. You will have to lay a foundation on self-awareness of your feelings, then begin to frame your home with words of encouragement, reflection, and understanding. Then you'll move on to installing your roof to seal things up and adding personal finishing touches inside your home. Think of this process as adding much-needed confidence boosters that will help to keep you standing strong. It may take time, but by the end you'll be proud of what you've built.

How to Manage This

A good way to manage how you build confidence is to keep a journal. If you're not the journaling-on-paper type, it's fine to use the note app on your smartphone in the same way. Reflect on things that boost your confidence and consider things that make you feel less confident. We've talked a lot about self-awareness in this chapter, but understanding how you feel and why you feel a certain way is helpful to your growth and key in building your self-confidence.

Write It Out

Fill in the chart about the current state of your self-confidence. Once you've finished, consider how you plan to address areas where you're less confident and increase time spent in areas where you are confident.

I FEEL CONFIDENT WHEN...	I DON'T FEEL CONFIDENT WHEN...	I CAN BUILD CONFIDENCE BY...

I FEEL CONFIDENT WHEN...	I DON'T FEEL CONFIDENT WHEN...	I CAN BUILD CONFIDENCE BY...

Action Steps

Now that you've reflected on your self-confidence, it's time to start building. Using the example of building a house, consider how you can build up your self-confidence by filling your life with ways you can succeed. It's also a good idea to consistently reevaluate areas or people that bring your confidence down. Are the things that bring you down really necessary? Where can you cut out those experiences? How can you maximize what makes you happy and confident?

What Role Do Insecurities Play in My Life?

Many mental health conditions, such as anxiety and depression, go hand in hand with insecurities. However, it's important to note that you don't have to have a diagnosed condition to be affected by insecurities. Insecurities prevent you from gaining the self-confidence you need to move forward or make change. Insecurity can show up via disappointment, self-doubt, and an uncertainty in your abilities. Therefore, you have to constantly be cognizant of insecurities and find ways to get rid of them. Insecurities will pop throughout life, so it's important for you to identify and address them before they hinder you.

How to Manage This

Insecurities are often built on a fear of failure. A great way to begin managing your insecurities is by first asking yourself *why* you're afraid to fail and *who* you're afraid to fail in front of. The answers to these questions may surprise you. However, this is the first step in discovering why you may be experiencing feelings of insecurity. As you reflect, continually focus on the truth that if you fail, not all is lost. You can get back up!

Write It Out

In this activity, let's think about three scenarios where you did not chase something that you wanted to pursue because of insecurities.

SCENARIO 1

What was something you missed out on because you felt insecure?

Why did you feel that way?

Do you regret the incident?

How have you grown past the feeling?

Looking back, is there anything you could change to make yourself more confident?

SCENARIO 2

What was something you missed out on because you felt insecure?

Why did you feel that way?

Do you regret the incident?

How have you grown past the feeling?

Looking back, is there anything you could change to make yourself more confident?

SCENARIO 3

What was something you missed out on because you felt insecure?

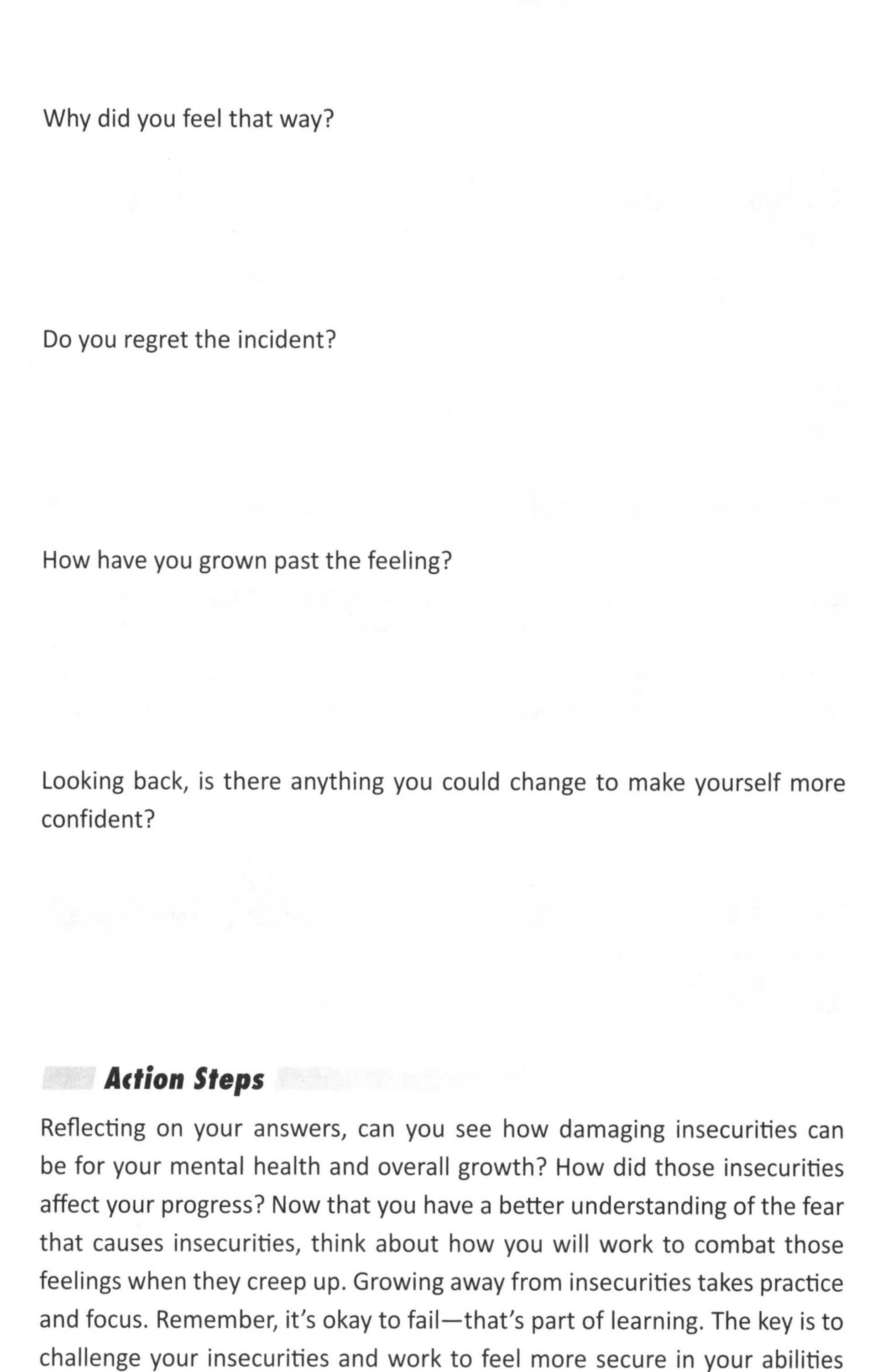

Why did you feel that way?

Do you regret the incident?

How have you grown past the feeling?

Looking back, is there anything you could change to make yourself more confident?

Action Steps

Reflecting on your answers, can you see how damaging insecurities can be for your mental health and overall growth? How did those insecurities affect your progress? Now that you have a better understanding of the fear that causes insecurities, think about how you will work to combat those feelings when they creep up. Growing away from insecurities takes practice and focus. Remember, it's okay to fail—that's part of learning. The key is to challenge your insecurities and work to feel more secure in your abilities and who you are.

Toss Failure Out the Window

As a child, you may have dreamed about what you'd do when you grew up. Maybe you wanted to be an astronaut or president. But as you get older, low self-confidence, a fear of embarrassment, failure, or even impostor syndrome can get in the way of your dreams. When you think of how you let those dreams go, you might feel sad or disappointed in your choices. Even if you don't go on to become president, you can still reclaim some of that fearlessness and confidence that you had as a child.

How to Manage This

One way to rebuild your confidence is to shift your mindset to imagine that failure isn't even a possibility. To start thinking this way, make a plan to do just one thing without fear. Taking action will jumpstart your plan and put you on the right path to success. Failure isn't a "bad" thing because you learn how to do things and what not to do. It also teaches you confidence because you tried something new and learned how to conquer it.

Write It Out

In this activity, write three things that you would do if you knew you could not fail. Start small. Maybe you want to create a piece of pottery or publish a poem on a public blog.

1. ______________________________

____

____

2. ______________________________

____

____

3. ______________________________

____

____

Now, to take it a step further, write down how you felt after doing each thing. Would you say your attempt was a success or a failure? How are you measuring those things? How could you improve your next attempt?

Action Steps

Reimagining failures as checkpoints on the way to success can help you get past a fear of failing. Plus, failing means that you've actually tried something! That requires bravery, confidence, and motivation—all things that you should celebrate. As you move forward, remember that failure is not a terrible thing. You may not get things exactly right the first time, but moving forward is filled with opportunities to try again and build confidence along the way.

Take Losses with Grace

Do you have a favorite sports team or player? If so, you know that they don't *always* win. Even the best teams are defeated at some point. However, they get back up and try again. They take their losses with a grain of salt. Being able to recognize that losses are a part of life and that we all have them will help you extend grace and empathy toward yourself. Instead of losing confidence because you lost, you want to be able to observe and appreciate what you learned from that loss so you can grow and improve.

How to Manage This

I used to have an extremely hard time as a child when I would lose a sporting event. I almost thought that it would be the end of the world to lose, and I would do anything to win. As an adult, I have realized that losing is a part of life. It's important to accept it as such, even while you continue working toward victory. No one *likes* losing, but if you can approach losses with an eye toward finding lessons and making improvements, you'll be much happier.

Write It Out

Write about the last time that you took a "loss" and how you handled it. Maybe you lost out on a promotion, or someone said no when you asked them out. How did you react?

Now explain how you could do things better next time.

Action Steps

This exercise will help you recognize that losing happens and it does not mean that you are any less of a person because you lost. Again, you can look at athletes as prime examples of people who take losses with dignity. They may not like it, but they move on and often come back stronger. Taking losses with grace is a skill that takes practice. You don't have to be an athlete to understand how to push forward through adversity. Keep moving forward—your next win could be right around the corner.

Visualize Success

Having a written reminder that you have succeeded before is very helpful. When you haven't felt successful in a while, it can be hard to remember what that's like! Instead of letting your confidence get dragged down, use this exercise to remind yourself what success feels like. Engaging with those sensations of success will boost your mood and confidence.

How to Manage This

Journaling, drawing, and writing are great ways of recording a permanent reminder of how you felt in a successful moment. It is so powerful to do this because you can always go back and see how you felt in that one moment, and that is a beautiful thing!

Write It Out

Write how you feel when you succeed, whatever success looks like to you. Success also can feel different with each win. You might feel like you're on top of the world, you can tackle anything, or you want to party! Fill in this chart to capture your observations.

WHAT DOES SUCCESS LOOK LIKE TO ME?	IN WHAT AREAS HAVE I BEEN SUCCESSFUL?	WHAT DO I DO WHEN I HAVE SUCCEEDED?	HOW DO I FEEL WHEN I HAVE SUCCEEDED?

WHAT DOES SUCCESS LOOK LIKE TO ME?	IN WHAT AREAS HAVE I BEEN SUCCESSFUL?	WHAT DO I DO WHEN I HAVE SUCCEEDED?	HOW DO I FEEL WHEN I HAVE SUCCEEDED?

Action Steps

Now that you've reflected on ideas surrounding success, it is a good idea to keep your observations at the front of your mind. Write your responses to what success looks like on a sticky note. Put those notes in places you pass by daily. This way, you have a reminder of what success looks like to you when you face adversity. Remember, success may look and feel different every day. For example, one day it may look like finding peace, and another day it may be completing a research paper. Whatever it is for you, it's important to remember it when obstacles get in your way.

The DL on Body Positivity

Appreciating your body is challenging for a lot of people. After all, the media are constantly bombarding us all with images of what the "perfect" body should look like. If you feel your body isn't what you want it to be, you might feel low self-esteem, shame, or feelings of worthlessness. These feelings will, of course, have a negative impact on your mental health and confidence levels. That's why it's important to work toward loving your body. An important note: If you find it especially challenging to find anything to love about your body, it may be time to get professional support.

How to Manage This

It will take time to begin to appreciate your body. There are many reasons why people don't love their body, and many of them are best worked on with a professional. Whether you find support groups that focus on body appreciation or try individual therapy, you want to be sure to have by your side people who are truly supportive of your authentic self.

Write It Out

This exercise is something you can try in order to get a sense of how you feel about your body. Try to ditch the criticisms, negative comparisons, and media ideals and, if possible, celebrate your amazing body. Write down something each body part does for you. For example, maybe your strong shoulders help you carry trays at your restaurant job. Maybe your hands allow you to paint beautiful images. Again, if this process is too difficult, seek support.

Hair:

Face:

Shoulders:

Hands:

Core:

Upper legs:

Lower legs:

Feet:

Action Steps

All too often, we criticize our bodies instead of celebrating them. Try to turn around that habit by rereading the things you wrote, especially when your body confidence is low. Your body is doing amazing things for you 24/7—you are breathing, circulating blood, and metabolizing nutrients without even *thinking* about it! Try to treat your body with the kindness, respect, and reverence it deserves.

Carrying Myself with Confidence

Remember that old phrase, "Dress for success"? The gist of that advice is to help you get into the mindset of success. While no one's saying that you need to wear a suit to every interview anymore, there is some wisdom in evaluating how you present yourself to the world. There are ways you can exude confidence using your posture and body language that both shows that confidence to others and helps you feel more confident as well.

How to Manage This

Exuding confidence takes practice. The way you enter a room, and move around the room, doesn't come naturally to many people. You can practice ways to exude confidence by looking in the mirror. Try different postures, facial expressions, and ways of greeting new people. Practice making speeches or giving presentations. You may feel uncomfortable the first few times, but after a few sessions, you'll begin to feel more confident and better able to project that feeling to others.

Write It Out

Let's do some mirror practicing. Try saying something, adjusting your posture, and jotting down how that felt. An example has been provided for you.

SAY	LOOK	FEEL
I am capable and confident today!	*Stand up as straight as you can, push your shoulders back.*	*When I do this, I feel like I can talk to anyone.*

SAY	LOOK	FEEL

Action Steps

You may look at politicians or personalities on TV and wonder how they became so confident. I assure you, most of them did not achieve it naturally! This exercise provides space to practice just like the pros do, and it is a good first step, but you could also do more research on this topic if it interests you. You can read books that focus on this particular skill and aid you as you move forward more confidently!

CHAPTER 7
SOCIAL CONNECTIONS

You can learn a lot about a person from the people they spend time with. Whether you notice it or not, you influence the people around you and vice versa. In a perfect world, you'd be surrounded by individuals who would push you to be the best version of yourself—both mentally and physically. Unfortunately, this isn't a perfect world. The good news is that you do have control over your environment, and there are things that you can do to dramatically change the quality of your social life.

Why is it important to have good people in your life? First of all, good friends bring joy and happiness into your life! Second, the people you surround yourself with can influence your mood, stress levels, and work-life balance and, as a result, impact your mental health. Interacting with trustworthy, kind, and friendly people will improve your mood. Finally, having the right people around you builds a community and a support system, which everybody needs for mental well-being.

In this chapter, you will learn about the different types of people you need in your life (such as family members, friends, loved ones, coworkers, and medical professionals). We'll focus on how it's the quality, not the quantity, of people that matters, and address how to minimize the impact of any toxic people in your circle. You'll learn how to be a good friend yourself and how to set boundaries when you need to. Let's begin working to help build that foundation for you!

Who's on My Team?

Every successful individual has a team of people to support them, guide them, and contribute to their success. When it comes to your mental health journey, it's helpful to have this team to keep you upright and help you "win" every day. Your teammates might include your parents, friends, coworkers, therapists, counselors, doctors—or a combination of these individuals (it can even include me, with my online help!). People who have a strong support network tend to feel happier and more confident.

How to Manage This

Each person's team is going to look different, but the key is that your team should support your specific needs and consist of people you can trust. Growing up, I was a huge sports fan and saw that every championship team was different: Some had great defenses, others had good offenses, and some were a mix of each. But they were all champions! It's time to think about who's on the roster of *your* championship team.

Write It Out

Make a list of the people who support you, and how they do so. For example, "Dr. Jones: makes sure I stay healthy." "Sean: always listens and lifts my spirits."

PERSON	HOW THEY SUPPORT ME

PERSON	HOW THEY SUPPORT ME

Action Steps

Look over your list. Take a moment to feel grateful for all the amazing people you have in your life. (Have you told them how amazing they are lately?) Now ask yourself if there is anyone missing. Do you have a mental health professional? A career mentor? A friend who shares your hobbies? Who else would be a good asset to your team? During the next month, see if you can recruit a few more team members to join you on your mental health journey.

What Kind of Friend Am I?

Humans are complex, and it can be difficult to know how to support your friends, especially when you have needs as well. Maybe your good friend needs a shoulder to cry on, or just a listening ear. Or maybe your friend needs someone to physically be there while they're going through a crisis. It's easy to get caught up in your own issues and not be emotionally or physically available to nurture your friendships. But not being a good friend can cause issues to your mental health, as well as isolate you from making strong connections. Keep in mind that being a good friend can be helpful for you too—fulfilling friendships provide positive emotions and a heightened sense of purpose and value.

How to Manage This

It was important for me to make stronger connections by creating a safe space for my friend group. The safe space enabled my friends to feel comfortable reaching out and allowed all of us to be authentic. Creating an environment where people can be authentic gives you a chance to connect with others on a more personal level and nurture stronger connections. It's also a part of being a good friend.

Write It Out

For this exercise, think about situations you might have with a friend and how you can react in a way that provides that person with a safe space to be their authentic self. Look over this checklist and check off any behaviors you already have. Feel free to add your own reactions in the blank spaces.

- ❑ Listening carefully (for example, not looking at your phone while they talk)
- ❑ Being patient while they speak (not interrupting)
- ❑ Offering empathy
- ❑ Sharing enthusiasm

- ❑ Acting nonjudgmentally
- ❑ Being kind and caring
- ❑ Checking to see if they want advice before you offer it
- ❑ Asking follow-up questions
- ❑ ____
  ____
- ❑ ____
  ____
- ❑ ____
  ____
- ❑ ____
  ____
- ❑ ____
  ____
- ❑ ____
  ____

Action Steps

Any behaviors you *didn't* check are good areas for you to improve on in the future. If in the past you'd interrupt someone to offer your take on the situation, maybe next time you can sit back, listen, and ask questions instead. Friendship groups should encourage each other and nurture positive relationships. To do that, friends must create a safe environment to express themselves, grow, and support one another. In completing this exercise, you might have been reminded of a time you *weren't* a perfect friend. That's okay—what's important is that you learned and can do better next time. As you focus on your mental health, you'll likely find that your best relationships grow even deeper and stronger because of the work you're doing!

How Do I Speak to Others?

Sometimes the way we speak to others is a reflection of how we feel about ourselves. I think of this often when I get a "hate" comment online or someone calls me a name. I take a moment to think about the hurt that they may be carrying, which is being reflected in their words. When you are speaking out of love, however, your words can uplift a person, make their day a little better, or even help someone who is struggling with social anxiety. Brightening someone else's day is a powerful boost to your confidence and mood as well.

How to Manage This

There are days when it takes more effort for me to get conversational with people. I could have had difficulties with my day or maybe I'm running behind on tasks....You might know the feeling. These things happen, and feelings like this are valid. However, it is still important to treat people with kindness, respect, and dignity—regardless of what is happening with you internally. Try taking a deep breath, temporarily setting aside your minor issues, and focusing on your friend.

Write It Out

Imagine that you're meeting a friend who is going through a hardship or a trying experience. What are some kind words you can offer in comfort or support? For example, "I'm so sorry this is happening to you." Write down your thoughts.

Now take those words and come up with a script using them in an encouraging conversation with a friend. Think about your friend's needs, ensuring a safe space and creating a positive discussion.

Action Steps

The way you speak to people matters—it tells others the type of person you are. Plus, treating people the way you want to be treated is a simple way to position yourself to have the same energy reciprocated back to you. The next time a friend needs help, try to remember these words you wrote and offer them in a nonjudgmental, supportive way. Just keep in mind that your needs are important too. If you're feeling overwhelmed at that moment and can't take on someone else's difficulties, it's okay to say that and ask to catch up at a different time.

Intentional Acts of Kindness

If you struggle to recognize your worth, you might experience feelings of insecurity, self-doubt, or helplessness that can lead to depression. Doubting your place in the world is very damaging to your mental health. If you feel this way, be sure that you are seeing a professional who can help you. This exercise will walk you through one simple way to recognize your worth. If it is insufficient, you may need to seek additional support or professional help as well.

How to Manage This

Doing nice things for others—whether people you know or strangers—is a powerful way to appreciate the impact you can have on the world around you. There's a pure feeling that you get when you do something selflessly. As a child, I would open the door for an elderly person, and my mom would react as if I'd just won the national spelling bee! Unfortunately, I often notice a sense of worthlessness in many of my patients who struggle with depression. They think that they have no value in the world. If you're struggling with similar thoughts, know that you do have value. One way to counteract those feelings is by being kind to others and recognizing the impact of your good deeds. With time, you'll recognize the fact that you belong. You matter. We need you in the world!

Write It Out

Check off some of the acts of kindness you'd like to try. Then write down your own ideas for intentional acts of kindness.

- ❑ Buy a coffee for the person behind you in line.
- ❑ Send a friend a card in the mail.
- ❑ Give a stranger a compliment.
- ❑ Bring flowers to a coworker.
- ❑ Do yard work for an elderly neighbor.

- ❑ Paint a small rock with a kind message and leave it where others will see it.
- ❑ Add money to an expired parking meter.
- ❑ Bake cookies for first responders.
- ❑ Tip your server extra well.
- ❑ ____________________
- ❑ ____________________
- ❑ ____________________
- ❑ ____________________
- ❑ ____________________
- ❑ ____________________
- ❑ ____________________
- ❑ ____________________

Action Steps

Over the next week, try to do one or two of these kind things for others as you continue your mental health journey. They will bring joy to people—and will help you feel a sense of purpose too. You'll probably find that you want to keep doing more and more because of the good vibes you're spreading! It's a beautiful feeling for both parties.

Trusting My Gut

Have you ever had a bad feeling about someone and later realized you were right? When it comes to decision-making and surrounding yourself with the best possible people for your needs, it's important to listen to your instincts. Pay attention to what makes you feel uncomfortable, and trust your gut when you feel uneasy around people. Recognizing patterns in other people's behavior can help you avoid negative feelings that can affect your mental health. For example, if someone doesn't respect your boundaries or seem to care about you, you might want to limit the amount of time you spend with them.

How to Manage This

Depending on where you are on your mental health journey, you may want to completely avoid certain people who make you uncomfortable. For example, if you know someone is always overly negative, you may be left feeling down after you're around them. If you're trying to be positive, this kind of interaction can set you back in your journey. If you feel confident enough in yourself and your needs, you probably don't have to cut out people altogether, but you'll need to be careful not to let their negativity rub off on you. Either way, you want to be sure you're listening to that inner voice and noticing red flags in people's behavior.

Write It Out

It can be hard to define what makes us uncomfortable—we usually just know it when we see it. So instead, write down "green flags" that make you feel good about a person. For example: "patient," "kind." Write why those qualities make you feel safe and secure. When you can identify and define these green flags, you'll know even better if you're not seeing them in a particular person. For example, "I like when a person is patient because I feel like I can take my time talking to them, and they act like my words are important to them."

Action Steps

I hope you run into many more of these green flags than you do red ones. But when you do encounter someone whose vibe doesn't match yours, trust your instincts. Politely excuse yourself, or say goodbye, or end the date—whatever it takes. It's not worth subjecting yourself to behavior that doesn't match the goals you have for your mental health. The key is trusting your gut in these moments so you can make good decisions about who you spend your time with.

Toxic Behavior 101

Dealing with your friends' behavior is extra tricky. We're not talking about strangers you can just walk away from or a blind date you can end early—these may be people you've known for years. Look, *everyone* has undesirable or even potentially toxic traits. No one is perfect, and this is true of yourself and the people you deal with. You should always keep that in mind. However, as you prioritize your needs and mental health, you may begin to spend less time with some individuals in your life. For example, if a good friend of yours is asking you to participate in an activity that they enjoy but is not good for your mental health journey, then it may be a good idea to decline the invitation.

How to Manage This

If you notice a pattern of negative behaviors that occur with certain people you spend time with, then it may be a good idea to reevaluate that friendship. You may want to ask yourself, "Am I gaining anything positive from this friendship?" If you are, can you enjoy their time in a different way? And I know it can be really hard to do this sometimes, but remember this: Nothing is more important than your mental health! For example, if you are trying to drink alcohol less often and one friend always wants to go out drinking, maybe you two could instead meet up for a bike ride, since you both love biking.

Write It Out

List some activities your friends do that could hinder your mental health journey. For example: participating in gossip. Pay attention to these things when engaging with friends or romantic relationships.

Now let's brainstorm how to tell your friends about your new focus on mental health. For example, if your friend invites you out for drinks, you might say, "Oh man, I used to love going to parties on Saturday nights! But I am trying to drink less often now. It was messing with my body too much. Hey, I saw you biking at Overlook Trail—want to meet me there Saturday afternoon for a ride instead?" Write what you could say here.

Action Steps

Understanding toxic behavior that may hinder your mental health journey is very important. When you identify actions that may negatively impact you, you'll find it easier to choose your friends, plans, and surroundings more carefully. I'm not saying it's easy to make these changes, especially with friends you have known for a long time, but sometimes you have to make tough choices on this mental health journey. Even if you experience some short-term pain with certain friends, keep reminding yourself that putting your needs and health first is always the right decision.

How to Have a Difficult Conversation

Difficult conversations can be draining and uncomfortable. They can make people angry, sad, or downright mean. That's why so many people avoid them! However, when you avoid these conversations, things that are left unsaid can build up and create chronic stress, anxiety, and frustration, all of which negatively impact your mental health. Avoidance also could lead to years of miscommunication and unwarranted anger or guilt. It's important to advocate for yourself, and having difficult conversations does just that.

How to Manage This

Having difficult conversations may feel scary at first, but there are ways to prepare yourself ahead of time. First, determine what you want to discuss and then stay focused on the solution. Once you create a plan, it's easier to manage the conversation and move past any uncomfortable feelings because you have a road map in mind. Having the courage to talk about tough topics will allow you to better advocate for yourself and improve your communication skills. These conversations are hard, and having them shows growth in your journey.

Write It Out

For the first part of this activity, identify one or two conversations that are often difficult for you, and why. For example, "I'm uncomfortable speaking to my manager because I'm afraid she doesn't think I'm doing a good job." Or, "I don't like telling my mother I don't want to take her advice because she'll tell me I'm making a mistake."

Now let's dig a little deeper and write down why it is important to have these conversations even if they're difficult. For example, "It's important to have open lines of communication with my boss so that if she does have feedback, I can receive it and act on it." Or, "I want my mom to know I value her advice, but I also want to make my own choices."

Action Steps

Completing this activity will allow you to have better insight into the reasons you may be fearful of having difficult conversations—and why you should have them anyway. Reflect on why you consider these conversations difficult and how you can break through that fear. Spending a bit of time reflecting and preparing is also a good way to manage the fear, anxiety, or even panic associated with facing difficult conversations. With a clear plan—and practice—you will grow more confident in approaching conversations that you once considered difficult. Communication skills are such an important part of maintaining strong relationships—whether personal, romantic, or professional—and the results will be worth your effort.

Finding My Crowd

We've discussed the joy and positivity attached to helping others and volunteering your time. But community engagement is a little different. We all come from different communities, spiritual traditions, or cultures. Many of us have a deep connection to our communities, whether the experience was positive or negative. If you grew up in an unsupportive or toxic group, it's important to leave that one behind and instead create or join the type of community you *do* want to live in. And if you have fond memories or current happy experiences with your community, it's important to maintain that sense of connection. Belonging to a cultural group is good for your mental health because it helps solidify your identity, gives you a sense of community spirit, and is just plain fun!

How to Manage This

Getting involved in the cultural, spiritual, or community organization that you identify with helps you stay connected to that group. You may want to attend special events or regular services or meetings, help out in some way, or try to meet new people there. I stay involved at my local church by offering free guitar lessons and organizing youth basketball games. These activities allow me to do things I love while connecting with others in my community.

Write It Out

For the first part of this exercise, think of groups you want to belong to. These could be groups you've been part of your whole life, or new ones that you identify with now that you are an adult making your own decisions.

Now brainstorm how you could get involved. For example, you might start by following a group on social media to learn about upcoming events.

Action Steps

Creating these lists gives you ways to start connecting with your community immediately. Being part of a larger cultural group is especially important if you're part of a marginalized community. It's vital to know your voice is important and you're not alone. Your mental health will be bolstered by this strong sense of belonging and community.

Making New Friends

Making a new friend can create genuine feelings of excitement. But making friends as an adult might feel much more difficult than it did when you were a kid. Why is that? You might be holding onto some social anxiety, fears of being accepted, or self-doubt. Despite those challenges, it's important to continue to make new connections throughout your life. After all, you're not exactly the same now as you were when you were seven. Your social circle should reflect that growth.

How to Manage This

Most friendships are started by simple conversations at the right moment. I met my best friend Mike when he asked to sit next to me in the lunchroom. Turns out, we had similar interests and a friendship was born. Putting yourself out there can seem difficult as an adult, so try starting a conversation with someone in a place that feels safe to you. If interests align, you could be on your way to creating a friendship.

Write It Out

For this exercise, describe what happened the last time you made a new friend.

How did it make you feel? Nervous, excited, sad? Why?

What did you find difficult about the experience?

What did you like about the experience?

Using your answers as a guide, think about ways you can feel more comfortable when making connections with potential friends. Maybe you enjoy meeting new friends within the safety of your current group of friends. Or maybe you prefer to make connections virtually instead of in person. Be honest with yourself so you can determine which activities or interactions trigger anxiety or negative emotions.

Action Steps

Now that you have evaluated how you feel when making a new friend, if you think those are manageable emotions, start a conversation with someone new. See if you feel the emotions you thought you would have, and if they match up to what you experience. If you are unsure about starting a random conversation with a stranger, do it in a safer space, like at a gathering of friends or a work function where you can meet new people.

Embracing the Single Life

In today's world, it is so difficult to not compare yourself to other people. Unfortunately, these comparisons often lead to insecurities, self-loathing, and even depression. For example, being single can be tough on someone's mental health because pressure from social media, peers, and friends may make you question your self-worth if you happen to be without a partner. Of course, there is nothing wrong with being single, and you should love yourself both when you're with a partner and when you're on your own.

How to Manage This

A good way to manage being single is just to embrace it! We can lean into ourselves more, and this stance helps us have more of a balance when we do enter into a relationship! Take a step back and focus on yourself for just a little bit. Remind yourself that you are a human being who is worthy of love, attention, respect, and so much more—just as you are.

Write It Out

For this activity, think of three things that you enjoy, that may be *better* to do while you are single. For example, maybe your partner doesn't usually like the same kind of movies you like—if so, going to the movies might be more fun alone.

1. ______________________________

____

____

2. ______________________________

____

____

3. ____

____

____

Action Steps

This list will help you seize the moment and have fun being single. Like so many things in life, changing your perspective is a powerful way to improve your outlook—and your mood and mental health will follow. Instead of feeling bad that you are single, transform your mindset and enjoy spending time with an amazing partner—yourself!

Managing Your Mental Health While in a Relationship

Being in a relationship is great for so many reasons—you're with someone you're compatible with, having a great time. But along with these good times come some trickier moments because now you are exposed to the emotions and the well-being of another individual on a more intimate level. When this happens, some people find themselves neglecting their own needs and overly focusing on their partner. Although, of course, you want to support your partner emotionally, it's important not to lose sight of your own needs and feelings either.

How to Manage This

You can keep your own needs at the forefront in a relationship by learning how to speak up for yourself (and encouraging your partner to do the same). Ongoing communication will help you air problems and work through trouble spots. People who are naturally more quiet or shy might find this pattern uncomfortable at first, but sharing your feelings, worries, and concerns can help you grow as a couple and make the relationship even stronger.

Write It Out

For this activity, think about your current relationship. First, write down three things that are going well for you.

1. ______________________________

2. ______________________________

3. ______________________________

Be sure to celebrate those things! Now list three parts of the relationship that you want to improve. Maybe you're always hanging out with their friends, or your partner cuts you off when you're trying to vent about your tough day.

1. ____

____

2. ____

____

3. ____

____

Finally, brainstorm ways that you can advocate for these improvements respectfully with your partner. For example, you could say, "I really like hanging out with your crew, but I've been missing mine lately! Can we grab dinner with them on Saturday instead of meeting your friends again?"

1. ____

____

2. ____

____

3. ____

____

Action Steps

This exercise can help you both identify your needs in the relationship *and* communicate to your partner about them. It is my hope that once you do this, you will not only advocate for yourself more but also be in a better position to emotionally provide for your partner. When you feel valued and worthy, you are more likely to help others feel that way too. The next time you find yourself upset about something going on in your relationship, reflect on how it could be improved, then talk about it calmly with your partner. Stewing in anger or acting passive-aggressive doesn't solve any problems—but talking about them can!

Setting Healthy Boundaries

Boundaries sometimes get a bad rap. For example, they imply that you're nervous, vulnerable, selfish, or pushy. Nothing could be further from the truth! Boundaries are simply guidelines that you set for how you want to be treated. From work relationships to personal relationships, you have to be assertive about your wants and needs. When you don't set boundaries, people can take more from you than you have to give. That imbalance can create chronic stress and anxiety, feelings of burnout, and frustration.

How to Manage This

Setting boundaries can be challenging at first if you've never done it before. It's important to remember that simply stating your boundaries is not rude or scary. You don't have to feel bad or guilty about expressing your needs. If you struggle with being assertive, know that this skill will improve with continued practice. Take small steps by starting in areas that are more comfortable to you. Are you comfortable speaking to your coworkers? Start there. If not, maybe try this out with your group of friends. You'll soon develop confidence that will help you be more successful in various areas of your life.

Write It Out

For this activity, list three areas where you think you need a boundary. Maybe you're dealing with a pushy boss, a toxic cousin, or an overbearing parent. Think about situations that stress you out—that stress is a good indicator that a boundary is needed.

1. ______________________________

____

2. ______________________________

____

3. ____

____

Now jot down seven things that make you feel confident and assertive. For example, practicing what you'll say ahead of time, wearing a certain outfit, or repeating an affirmation might help you feel empowered.

1. ____

____

2. ____

____

3. ____

____

4. ____

____

5. ____

____

6. ____

____

7. ____

____

Finally, put the two lists together and brainstorm exactly how you can state your needed boundaries to the appropriate person. Maybe you can jot down a few sentences ahead of time, wear that new shirt, or ask your boss to please stop calling you every night because that's your personal time.

1. ____

____

2. ____

____

3. ____

____

4. ____

____

5. ____

____

Action Steps

Try to implement one or two of these ideas the next time you need to assert yourself. You'll feel prepared and set yourself up for success. Return to your list once in a while to add or adjust what works for you. Feel free to use extra paper to brainstorm the next time you need to plan what you want to say. Remember, becoming more assertive won't happen overnight, but setting boundaries is an important part of maintaining good mental health as you navigate relationships with others.

CONCLUSION

Wow! You have come such a long way on your journey. You should be so proud of your progress. We've discussed many important ways to improve your mental health. From dealing with sadness, to understanding when to seek professional help, to setting boundaries and building your confidence, this book has given you dozens of tools to use as you continue your mental health journey.

Your journey isn't over, of course. Observing and improving your mental health is a lifelong goal that everyone can always be working on. As you continue your journey toward wellness, take time to reflect on and reread the activities you completed in this workbook. You may need to revisit certain topics as reminders or to help you during challenging times. However you use this book in the future, remember that it is here to help you move forward.

As you worked through this book, you likely found yourself becoming more confident and comfortable talking about mental health. If so, you might want to consider becoming a mental health advocate. What does that mean? Simply spreading awareness about mental health by speaking openly and positively about mental health topics. Doing this is a great way to overcome stigma *and* advocate for yourself and others. It may be uncomfortable at first, but I want you to know that doing your best is good enough. We all have to start somewhere, and using this workbook is a great place to begin!

RESOURCES

Following are some key resources you can use to get even more information about your mental health. You'll find descriptions of each group, sometimes in their own words, along with contact information.

AAKOMA Project

The AAKOMA Project's mission is to "build the consciousness of Youth of Color and their caregivers on the recognition and importance of mental health, empowering youth and their families to seek help and manage mental health and influence systems and services to receive and address the needs of Youth of Color and their families."

 **(571) 486-3382**

 ***https://aakomaproject.org***

American Foundation for Suicide Prevention (AFSP)

The AFSP seeks to prevent suicide and provides support to those who have lost (or almost lost) someone to suicide. With chapters in each of the fifty US states, it aims to "take action against this leading cause of death."

 **(888) 333-2377**

 ***https://afsp.org***

American Psychological Association (APA)

The APA reports that it "is the leading scientific and professional organization representing psychology in the United States, with more than 133,000 researchers, educators, clinicians, consultants, and students as its members."

 **(800) 374-2721 OR (202) 336-5500**

 ***www.apa.org***

Anxiety and Depression Association of America (ADAA)

The ADAA is a nonprofit organization that focuses primarily on anxiety disorders and depression. Its mission is to improve the quality of life for people who suffer from these disorders, by providing research, facts, and resources.

(240) 485-1001

https://adaa.org

Anxiety Network

The Anxiety Network focuses on panic disorder, generalized anxiety disorder, and social anxiety disorder. It provides facts, information, and personal blog posts to help people overcome these three disorders.

https://anxietynetwork.com

Born This Way Foundation

The Born This Way Foundation advocates for mental wellness and empowerment. It focuses on young people, emphasizing their creativity, diversity, and potential. Its mission is "to build a kinder and braver world."

https://bornthisway.foundation

Centers for Disease Control and Prevention (CDC)

The CDC is the national public health agency of the United States. It is a US federal agency under the Department of Health and Human Services, and is headquartered in Atlanta, Georgia.

(800) 232-4636

www.cdc.gov

Centre for Addiction and Mental Health (CAMH)

The CAMH is Canada's largest mental health teaching hospital and one of the world's leading research centers in its field. It is fully affiliated with the University of Toronto and is a Pan American Health Organization/World Health Organization Collaborating Centre.

 **(416) 535-8501**

 ***www.camh.ca***

Crisis Text Line

Crisis Text Line is a global nonprofit organization that provides free mental health texting services through confidential crisis intervention via text message. The organization's services are available 24/7 throughout the US, Canada, UK, and Ireland. Text HOME to 741741 for help.

 ***www.crisistextline.org***

#HalfTheStory

#HalfTheStory's mission is to "empower the next generation's relationship with social media, through advocacy, education, and providing access to resources for youth."

 ***https://halfthestoryproject.com***

Hope for Depression Research Foundation (HDRF)

The HDRF is a nonprofit organization that focuses on depression and related mood disorders. The foundation uses neuroscience research to study depression, its causes, new treatments, and methods of prevention. It also aims to eliminate the stigma surrounding depression.

 **(212) 676-3200**

 ***www.hopefordepression.org***

The Jed Foundation

The Jed Foundation is a nonprofit organization that protects emotional health and works to prevent suicide among teens and young adults in the United States.

 **(212) 647-7544**

 ***https://jedfoundation.org***

LGBT National Help Center

The LGBT National Help Center provides "free and confidential telephone and internet peer-counseling information and local resources for gay, lesbian, bisexual, transgender and questioning caller throughout the United States."

 **(888) 843-4564**

 ***www.glbtnationalhelpcenter.org***

Mental Health America (MHA)

MHA is "the nation's leading community-based nonprofit dedicated to addressing the needs of those living with mental illness and promoting the overall mental health of all."

(703) 684-7722

https://mhanational.org

Mental Health Resources (MHR)

MHR is "a progressive, nonprofit organization that offers community-based mental health and substance use disorder services to adults recovering from serious mental illness."

(651) 659-2900

www.mhresources.org

The MINDS Foundation

The MINDS Foundation, a nonprofit organization located in India, uses a grassroots approach to eliminate stigma and provide educational, medical, and moral support for people with mental illness in rural India.

(424) 646-3704

www.mindsfoundation.org

MindWise—Military and Family Screenings

MindWise offers behavioral health screenings for military members and families. This program is anonymous and confidential. After completing a brief questionnaire, participants can view their results, recommendations, and key resources.

https://screening.mentalhealthscreening.org/Military_NDSD

National Alliance on Mental Illness (NAMI)

NAMI is "the nation's largest grassroots mental health organization dedicated to building better lives for the millions of Americans affected by mental illness."

 **(800) 950-6264**

 ***www.nami.org***

National Council for Mental Wellbeing

The National Council for Mental Wellbeing is "a membership organization that drives policy and social change on behalf of over 3,100 mental health and substance use treatment organizations and the more than 10 million children, adults and families they serve. We advocate for policies to ensure equitable access to high-quality services. We build the capacity of mental health and substance use treatment organizations. And we promote greater understanding of mental wellbeing as a core component of comprehensive health and health care. Through our Mental Health First Aid (MHFA) program, we have trained more than 2.6 million people in the U.S. to identify, understand and respond to signs and symptoms of mental health and substance use challenges."

 **(202) 684-7457**

 ***www.thenationalcouncil.org***

National Institute of Mental Health (NIMH)

The NIMH is "the lead federal agency for research on mental disorders." It is one of the twenty-seven institutes and centers that make up the National Institutes of Health (NIH), the largest biomedical research agency in the world and part of the US Department of Health and Human Services.

 **(866) 615-6464**

 ***www.nimh.nih.gov***

spaceMVMNT

spaceMVMNT's mission is to "help individuals thrive by lowering the barriers to access and practice mental, physical and spiritual wellness with intention, inclusion and purpose." Its spaceMIND initiative "provides free, weekly emotional support groups in Los Angeles and virtually across the globe. We facilitate do-good, feel-good service projects to enhance our community by creating and organizing events with passion and purpose, to cultivate culture within our space. We believe in the power of human connection and how it will revitalize the impact in the work we are doing."

 ***www.spacemvmnt.com***

Substance Abuse and Mental Health Services Administration (SAMHSA)

The SAMHSA collects information on thousands of state-licensed providers who specialize in treating substance use disorders, addiction, and mental illness.

 **(800) 662-4357**

 ***https://findtreatment.gov***

Trevor Project

The Trevor Project is an American nonprofit organization that focuses on suicide prevention efforts among lesbian, gay, bisexual, transgender, queer, and questioning youth. Through a toll-free telephone number, it operates the Trevor Lifeline, a confidential service that offers trained counselors.

 **(866) 488-7386** OR TEXT **START** TO **678-678**

 ***www.thetrevorproject.org***

ULifeline

ULifeline is "an anonymous, confidential, online resource center, where college students can be comfortable searching for the information they need and want regarding emotional health."

 **(800) 273-8255**

 ***www.ulifeline.org***

US Department of Veterans Affairs Mental Health Resources

The Department of Veterans Affairs Mental Health Resources provides information about mental health and support services to veterans.

 **(877) 222-8387**

 ***www.mentalhealth.va.gov***

INDEX

A

B

C

H

I

J

K

L

M

T

ABOUT THE AUTHOR

DR. KOJO SARFO, DNP, PMHNP-BC, is a social media content creator, mental health nurse practitioner, and psychotherapist with more than three million followers across his social media platforms. He is also the host of *What's Good with Dr. Kojo*, a mental health podcast.

He posts skits, songs, and videos in order to bring people together and promote mental health awareness. On his *TikTok* channel, he uses relevant trends and popular music to educate individuals about mental health conditions and the importance of self-care. Dr. Sarfo is also the author of another book entitled *You Already Won*. Find him:

- **@drkojosarfo** on ***Instagram, Twitter, Twitch,*** and ***Facebook***
- **kojosarfo** on ***YouTube***
- **@dr.kojosarfo** on ***TikTok***